# THE

# 7

# STEPS

## TO

# PERFECT HEALTH

AVAILABLE NOW

The Ultimate Dinosaur
Robert Silverberg, Editor

Are We Alone in the Cosmos?
The Search for Alien Contact in the New Millennium
Ben Bova and Byron Preiss, Editors

The New Dinosaurs
by William Stout

Eclipse
Voyage to Darkness and Light
by David H. Levy

Scientific American
Guide to Science on the Internet
Edward Renahan

Scientific American's The Big Idea
David H. Levy, Editor

Space: The Next Business Frontier
Lou Dobbs with HP Newquist

Starry Night:
How to Skywatch in the 21st Century
John Mosley

# THE
# 7
# STEPS
# TO PERFECT HEALTH

## By
# Gary Null

**ibooks**
new york
www.ibooksinc.com
DISTRIBUTED BY SIMON & SCHUSTER, INC.

***LiveREADS*™**
*New York*

ibooks, inc.
24 West 25th Street
New York, NY 10010

The ibooks World Wide Web Site Address is:
http://www.ibooksinc.com


You can visit the ibooks Web site for a free read and
download of the first chapters of all the ibooks titles:
http://www.ibooksinc.com

ISBN 0-7434-4479-5
First ibooks, inc. printing December 2001
10 9 8 7 6 5 4 3 2 1

Cover design by carrie monaco
Interior design by Christopher Grassi

Printed in the U.S.A.

# Table of Contents

# THE 7 STEPS TO PERFECT HEALTH

# Step #1:

## Beginning the Road to Wellness

This is a program for wishing yourself well. It's about opening yourself up to positive energy instead of focusing on the negative. Given the fact that whatever you invest with energy increases its power, when you build on feeling good about your life and health, you'll become healthier. Conversely, if you're preoccupied with fighting off illness and stress, you'll feel stress and ill health.

How does this translate in practical terms? It means moving toward having strong stamina instead of always feeling fatigued and exhausted; it means that when you have a cold it only lasts a few days instead of months; it means having energy for life instead of constantly dragging yourself to doctors for chronic problems; it means taking time for yourself instead of always thinking you have to do more for others.

As long as disease and depression are getting more of your energy than wellness and happiness, the problematic aspects of your life will only continue. That's when ill health starts to spread and take over your world.

It has taken me a lifetime to learn this.

## *You're Not Being Deprived,*
## *You're Gaining Well-Being*

Changing your habits is a wonderful, exhilarating process, and the results reward the effort. It's not easy. We often give up because we're so accustomed to our life habits; we're on automatic pilot when we order a steak with French fries (leaving out the vegetables) and Death-by-Chocolate for dessert. Change requires accepting a different mindset about the way you eat which you may not, at first, completely subscribe to or understand—or like. Change takes time and effort. Not being able to have those foods we like and are used to makes us feel deprived. But once you have grown tired enough of the way you feel and learn the sound basis for these dietary and lifestyle suggestions, you'll be inspired to change. Further, once you feel the sense of well-being, increased energy, stamina, and mental clarity, experience fewer colds and less pain through the delicious and health-giving wonders of grains, vegetables, juices, nuts and seeds, and other aspects of this program, you'll want to stay the course. Feeling great is the best reason to change.

### *How We Achieve Wellness*

*The 7 Steps to Perfect Health* is the program through which you can feel that coveted sense of well-being. It will *not* teach you how to cure diseases resulting from toxins; it *will* teach how to replace those toxins with life-giving energy and nutrients. But first, you have to look at what you're doing now to prevent wellness:

- Eating too many processed, refined foods, animal fats and sugar
- Consuming meat, poultry, and dairy products
- Drinking caffeine and alcohol
- Not drinking sufficient quantities of fluids daily such as clean water and vegetable juices
- Not getting the right nutrients into your body
- Not coping well with work and family problems
- Not being mindful of your own needs
- Not taking the time to be still in your busy life; you're overstressed

Chances are if you're not paying attention to the destructive aspects of your diet and lifestyle, you're not paying attention to what your body is telling you when you suffer from chronic back pain, gastrointestinal distress, constipation, insomnia, and the more serious conditions of heart disease, arthritis, diabetes, and cancer. When you suffer too much, your body and your unconscious mind are telling you to stop what you're doing, and change your habits. When you change your habits properly you can reverse deteriorating health and prevent chronic conditions from taking root. You will feel better.

## Foods that Hurt

Recently Dr. Neil Barnard, President of The Physcians Committee for Responsible Medicine, said, "There is no longer any doubt that a diet high in meat, dairy, sugar, refined and processed foods is responsible for the increase in degenerative disorders so prevalent among our population." Although I'm not happy with this fact, I am glad that the medical establishment is finally waking up to the toxic effects of many foods. It's taken years for this to happen.

The American diet is loaded with refined and processed foods. But the very nature of processing strips food of its nutrients through agitation, pressure, and extreme temperature changes. Many food companies try to compensate for this inferior food by so-called fortification, whereby small amounts of nutrients are replaced. In the end they may remove forty nutrients and all the enzymes, replacing them with ten. This does little good for us. The lack of essential nutrients in pastas, breads, sugar, and grains means your vital organs are not being fed foods they can use.

The problem with refined foods was dramatized in the 1970s when many Asian refugees were dying from Sudden Unexpected Death Syndrome. Originally the cause was thought to be the stress of adapting to a new culture, but upon closer examination it became clear that it was because their diet consisted mainly of refined white rice. In their native countries they were accustomed to eating whole grain rice which contains all the vital nutrients, including protein. However, processed white rice is virtually empty of nutritional value because the very important thiamine—which helps you heart pump properly—and vitamin B-1 have been removed. Processing may in addition kill off nutrients and food factors that have not yet been identified.

Low levels of selenium—which is stripped out of refined foods—have been correlated with cancer. Manganese deficiencies, which are rampant in America, are associated with irregular heartbeats, muscle fatigue, and insomnia.

Further exacerbating our health problems is that many

of us have been eating this way since infancy, when our foods were processed and pumped up with sugar. We grew up with a lifelong craving for these kinds of food products.

## Reconnecting to Natural Living

What contributes to a longer life? Reconnecting to a more natural way of eating and treating disease.

During childhood my family used many natural cures. I remember a time of a serious flu epidemic. As a preventive measure, my mother applied a mustard plaster—a vapor rub made of mustard and horseradish—to my chest. It burned and stung, but I didn't get sick. On a daily basis she'd also give me cod liver oil. I hated it. But now we know how rich cod liver oil is in vitamins A and D. My family also ate onions regularly to prevent illness. Whenever I had a high temperature, my mother would place an onion plaster on my forehead; she'd make a poultice from onion and garlic to bring fever down as well.

It seems that people once possessed a kind of innate wisdom about how to live long, healthy lives before the age of processed foods and chemicals. This simple wisdom, combined with all we know today about the value of juices and nutrients, makes us particularly well equipped to give ourselves longevity, energy, stamina, and a sense of well-being.

## Phytochemicals to Reverse the Aging Process

The curative powers of those mustard plasters my mother used was no accident. Powerful elements were at work. Healing is not just about overcoming degenerative diseases; it's about reversing the aging process, about rejuvenating. If refined foods can hurt you, natural foods can heal—and they are powerful.

Phytochemicals—which protect plants from harmful substances—are found in fruits and vegetables and help protect our bodies against viruses, bacteria, yeast, and molds. There are hundreds of phytochemicals within each fruit or vegetable, and each helps specific cells to do their job. For example, there are 150 phytochemicals in the fig, and one of them has been shown to prevent cancer. Green juices are filled with chlorophyll, a great blood cleanser. Orange foods such as carrots contain carotenoids, which are anticarcinogenic. Phytochemicals help our DNA, which means they actually can repair a damaged cell. When cells are damaged, they become weak links, ultimately causing the body to break down and speed up the aging process.

### Knowing Where You Stand Through Alternative Testing

To know how to detox and rebuild and rejuvenate, you need to know where you stand. Improper levels of various substances can interfere with enzyme systems. Susceptibility to food allergies can cause a multitude of ills.

For example, few people know their cholesterol level. More important, they may not know the right way to look at cholesterol. To properly evaluate your cholesterol, high- density lipoprotein (HDL) levels, which is "good" cholesterol, must be compared to the levels of low-density lipoprotein (LDL), "bad" cholesterol, the kind that can make you sick.

The experts in the field of alternative testing are *complementary* or *holistic* doctors. Complementary physicians are more interested in following your medical history in detail; they are concerned with the chronology of symptomatology. When did the symptoms start? How did the symptoms develop? The complementary physician tries to correlate specific symptoms with the physiology of the body. For this, according to Dr. Martin Feldman, a complementary physician, the right tests are critical. Some of the diagnostic tests performed by traditional physicians and complementary physicians overlap, such as scratch tests for allergies, but most are completely different, using not only different techniques but different clues to establish the origin of a problem. For example, a holistic physician would use saliva instead of the traditional blood testing to determine levels of DHEA, testosterone, or estrogen, or he might use some other frontier laboratory tests.

## Chronic Low Energy

We're going to look at the chronic condition of low energy to show what options are available in testing. The traditional physician in this case would test the blood for low thyroid function, anemia, and Epstein-Barr virus. That's as far as he or she might go. If the problem doesn't show up here, the doctor might then conclude that since the low energy is not showing itself in any of the above diseases, it might be due to "just an emotional condition" or depressive state. However, there are far more possibilities for chronic low energy.

### FOOD ALLERGIES

Food allergies or food over-tolerance are possible hidden causes for low energy. To determine if allergies to certain foods are at the root of a problem, your doctor would ask that you keep a food diary in order to see not only what kinds of food you're eating, but how much of each you consume. In some rare cases, severe allergies—commonly to nuts or fruits—can cause outbreaks of rash, itching, or, in more serious cases, difficulty breathing. More commonly, food allergies will manifest a few hours or even a day after consumption, which makes diagnosis more complicated. The physician will analyze the diary to consider whether you're eating a particular food to excess; perhaps you're eating wheat two, three, or four times a day. That tends to correlate with an over-tolerance to that wheat.

Perhaps you feel tired after eating a meal? This could result from a low blood sugar reaction to a particular food to which you may have an allergy; or, it could be due to an imbalance of glucose in your system.

All of these food reactions can be tested without a laboratory in a carefully monitored "trial and error" effort in which you eliminate a food for 5 to 12 days and then reintroduce it at a "model meal" to see what happens. In the laboratory, an advanced level of allergy is often determined by an Immune Globulin Type E test (IgE). Classical allergy treatment considers a substance an allergen only if there's an elevation in the IgE level. The IgG (another antibody test), however, is a more important measure because it can check allergy states that don't show up on the IgE test. Other food allergy tests can include: cytotoxic food tests (which are not widely available), and intradermal testing, whereby a small amount of the food antigen is injected into the skin and the reaction is measured with a ruler. The advantage here is that the tester can test a dilution of the antigen to determine what is an acceptable level of that substance.

## IMMUNE DISORDERS

The next area to look for causes of a low-energy state would be the immune system. The conventional method for checking immune levels is to check the CBC blood count. In a healthy person, white blood cell count should be above 4.0; any count below 3.5 of total white blood count would be considered an immune imbalance. Further, the lymphocyte percentage of the white count should be not more than 45 percent of the total. Any more would indicate an imbalance and indicate that the immune system is challenged.

An immune system problem can also show itself through acupuncture. A sophisticated medical office can test the thymus energy field via acupuncture using either electrical or other meridian testing.

If an immune problem does test positive, there are a number of fairly easy ways to rebuild it using fundamental nutrients: vitamins A, B-6, B-12, C, E, bioflavonoids, GLA (gamma-linolenic acid or evening primrose oil), essential fatty acids (found in sunflower oil), and the minerals zinc and selenium. There are also many herbs that support the immune system. Thymus extract is available over-the-counter and can effect major repairs to an immune system that has gone awry. If the lymphatic system is off, as indicated by excessive CBC levels, jumping on a trampoline is an excellent way to get levels back on track. Finally, clean, filtered water boosts the immune system as well.

## INFECTION

Infection can result in chronic low energy. Epstein-Barr virus testing has only recently become a standard medical procedure. Reading the tests properly is perhaps the most critical element for correct diagnosis. Many people test for elevated Epstein-Barr B virus antibodies through Immunoglobulin G (IgG) levels. Elevated levels denote prior exposure, from anywhere six months to ten years earlier. You could argue that the presence of IgG antibodies provides some protection against a new outbreak of Epstein-Barr. An elevated IgG indicates there is current, new activity indicating the viral infection is active, but at its early stage. This is treatable, but it is a more severe problem than the IgG numbers indicate.

Herpes 6 CMV and Herpes 2 should also be tested—in the same herpes profile panel—as should other infections beside viral ones such as *candida albicans*, a yeast-like fungus. Candida overgrowth is a major problem in America today, largely due to intake of improper foods. *Candida albicans* is a normal substance found in the intestinal tract. However, low immunity, excess sugar intake, or use of antibiotics can cause an overgrowth of candida, which can be a cause of low energy. This can be tested via sophisticated stool or anal swab analysis. Once the level is known, correction is easily achieved by improving the diet and lifestyle, or by taking caprillic acid, a natural substance, not an antibiotic such as nystatin or other antibiotics, which are over-prescribed and result in other problems.

PARASITES

Parasites are also becoming endemic in America and may contribute to a fatigue syndrome. Somewhat difficult to test, they can be tracked through stool samples or anal swabs.

### NUTRITIONAL DEFICIENCIES

Deficiencies in such nutrients as vitamin B-6, all B-complex vitamins, and especially vitamin B-12, can contribute to low energy. This can be tracked simply by looking at the CBC blood count. However, interpretation is everything: if the red blood cells are enlarged to where the MCV line (Mean Cropuscular Volume) is above 98 to 100, this is highly correlated with a B-12 deficiency. Treatment is easy and includes taking a B-12 lozenge. Since B-12 is difficult to absorb through the stomach, the lozenges are effective sublingually. Many people who are being misdiagnosed as depressed have this MCV elevation and therefore can be treated with B-12.

### HORMONES

Testing hormone levels as possible factors causing fatigue has not yet been accepted by conventional medicine. Saliva testing rather than blood testing is the most accurate measure of hormone levels because the hormones that emerge from saliva are active. The important hormones to test for are: estradiol level for women in menopause; DHEA to get a handle on adrenal function; cortisol, also for adrenal function; and testosterone. Saliva testing is a marvelous advance, and the data is far more accurate than data derived from blood tests.

### BIOLOGICAL TESTING

Did you know that chronological age does not necessarily correspond with biological age? You may be forty, but your cells and your biochemistry may be eighty. This can be tested. Generally, the biochemical tests that people should have include the following:

- Estrogen
- Testosterone
- DHEA
- Human Growth Hormone
- Thyroid
- Triglycerides
- Lipid Profile

### GLUCOSE AND CHOLESTEROL

These tests should be done during an eight-to-ten hour fast, otherwise glucose and cholesterol levels will be skewed. Properly interpreted cholesterol levels have to take in several factors: the total cholesterol and the subdivisions of HDL and LDL. The HDL, or good cholesterol, removes cholesterol from the cells and sends it back to the liver. By carrying around the bad LDL, HDL acts as a buffer for it, keeping it from causing mischief. A healthy cholesterol count should have a higher amount of HDL to LDL as part of the total count. The lower the ratio of LDL to HDL the better, with the optimum level approximately 2 to 1. The best way to raise HDL levels is through exercise. Aerobic exercise three times a week for 30 minutes is the minimum requirement to raise good cholesterol levels.

The glucose level has to be considered as only one moment in time; a fasting glucose level, for example, only tells part of the story, but it's a start. Laboratories will tell you that a normal glucose level is between 65 and 110. But that's wrong—your range should not go below 70 or over 105. Diabetes is defined at 145 or higher glucose. A traditional physician will accept a level of 115. A complementary medical physician would want to optimize that glucose and get it below 100.

THYROID

Thyroid testing, unfortunately, is incomplete. The Thyroid Stimulating Hormone (TSH) blood test is the most accurate of the three thyroid tests. As the thyroid is weakening, the pituitary gland has to give the thyroid more instructions about how to get going, thereby elevating the TSH; this is the first indication that there is a challenge to the thyroid. Easily 10 percent of the time, our thyroid gland is malfunctioning at some level. But that level is currently beyond our ability to test.

A better indicator for TSH than a blood test is the Barnes Metabolic Morning Temperature. In this test a thermometer is placed under the arm for ten minutes as you lay flat in bed. A temperature of over 97.6 indicates a normal thyroid level.

These are the basic tests for a chronic low-energy level. Tests exist for a variety of health issues. It's good to know what your levels are—though not absolutely necessary—when you begin a program of detoxification. In this way you'll know where you need more adjustments of nutrients, vitamins, enzymes, and other important health-giving substances for your body.

This is the beginning of a journey, the benefits of which you will only know as you start experiencing them by living differently than you do now. Once the rationale for greater health and how to achieve it are broken down for you, step by step, nothing will be overwhelming. You just have to stay the course.

## Step #2:

### *Eliminating Disease-Causing Agents*

We all want to feel our very best. But where can you turn for guidance on how to do it? Modern medicine doesn't seem to have the answer since it tends to focus not on feeling good but rather on what to do when you're already feeling bad. Our goal is *wellness:* how to feel great and prevent disease before it happens. The only way to prevent illness is to help our body take care of itself. We do that by enabling the organs that act as our body's detoxification system—the liver, kidneys, skin, and intestines—to do the job they were meant to do. Detoxifying our bodies, removing those foods and chemicals that don't belong in our system, is what helps our body work at its best. Later, I will show you how to replace those toxic substances with powerful nutrients, vitamins, herbs, juices, and other life-enhancing foods that give you energy, stamina, well-being—and keep you young.

Our first step toward wellness is to remove as many toxic agents as possible so that we can enjoy proper immune-system function, good digestion, and easy elimination. It will be difficult to rid ourselves of everything that challenges our systems; we can, however, focus on the worst offenders.

Twenty substances cause as much as 90 percent of the damage that's done to our bodies. Topping the list are refined foods and sugars. If a food is processed it no longer has nutritional value; it's dead, depriving the body of what it needs. It's the living energy in the food that does the healing. Food, in essence, is the missing link in disease.

### Sugar

Of all the refined foods we eat, sugar is the number-one culprit in causing such degenerative diseases as diabetes, hypoglycemia, obesity, tooth decay, gastrointestinal problems, aging, heart disease, cataracts, and cancer. In combination with a diet high in cholesterol and saturated fatty acids, sugar is a co-factor in heart disease.

Despite this knowledge, manufacturers routinely add sugar to just about everything because it's a cheap filler, and it adds flavor. You don't have to eat a teaspoon of sugar to be eating sugar; you get it when you eat just about anything: ketchup, soups, salad dressings, cakes, soft drinks, cookies, peanut butter, cheeses, canned and frozen vegetables, hamburgers, and corn syrups. Despite the many health disorders associated with sugar, the food industry promotes it as a pure, natural energy food.

When the body faces the challenge of handling sugar it will store it as fat. The home for these fat deposits is found in such low- exercised areas as thighs, buttocks, and breasts. When these storage areas reach their absorption capacity, the fat deposits then move into such major organs as the heart and kidneys, causing them to deteriorate and under-function.

## Diabetes

Among the most serious dangers of eating sugar is diabetes. In 1923, Dr. Frederick Banting won the Nobel Prize for his insulin extraction method. Even then, when Americans were consuming very little sugar, he noted that eating large quantities of sugar would increase the prevalence of diabetes. In his book, *Sugar Blues*, William Dufty compared the levels of diabetes in undeveloped societies that used unprocessed sugars versus more modern society using highly refined sugars. Not surprisingly, he found that in the first group the incidence of diabetes was low. But the moment these societies discovered how to boil down sugar cane, filter it, and use a bleaching agent to produce a pure, white crystalline sugar, the incidence of diabetes soared.

In babies, the action of insulin is seriously impaired when they're bottle-fed glucose or sugar water. The more sugar you consume the harder it is to maintain sugar balance, which leads to hypoglycemia or, worse, diabetes.

One of the first signs of a blood sugar disorder is fatigue, almost always followed by depression. When you're depressed and fatigued you eat more and become more sedentary, thereby gaining weight and elevating the possibility of diabetes and stroke.

Eliminating sugar from the diet, however, can result in powerful, positive change. A woman in one of my wellness groups who had a severe case of diabetes and was taking many drugs was able to go off all of her drugs and become stabilized just by eliminating sugar from her diet.

## Hyperactivity

Sugar's effect on behavior, particularly on children, has generated much concern. Studies performed at Yale University on children showed the stimulating effect of sugar on the adrenal gland to be a factor strongly correlated with hyperactivity and irritability. Likewise, a double-blind study showed inappropriate behavior in preschool children one hour after drinking a sweetened drink.

One woman whose two sons were suffering from Attention Deficit Disorder and being treated unsuccessfully with Ritalin found out how eliminating sugar could change their lives. After attending a program I offered on a sugar elimination diet, the woman applied the protocol to her children, eliminating not only all sugar but such sugar substitutes as aspartame and saccharine. Within three days her sons were out of control; the medications were not working. One son was sent home from school; neither could sleep, and there were endless arguments. They were clearly undergoing withdrawal, which was to be expected. I suggested she give them a program of herbs, vitamins, and nutrients; within two days, the boys calmed down. A week later, for the first time in five years, the children behaved normally and were able to slowly withdraw from their medications. Her physician husband didn't believe that removing sugar had been the cure for their sons' problems. To prove to him that it did, I suggested she give the boys some sugar and see what happened. She did, and soon they were bouncing off the walls—the symptoms had come back. No more proof was needed. She took a deep breath and said, "I got my sons back—and all because of eliminating the bad effects of sugar!"

## Periodontal Disease

In addition to tooth decay, sugar can lead to tooth loss by stripping the teeth of calcium. Six teaspoons of sugar will cause calcium to leach from the bones two hours after intake, which also contributes to osteoporosis.

## Osteoporosis

To show that sugar—and caffeine—in the diet eliminates calcium, I worked with a group of postmenopausal women who had osteoporosis and were taking calcium tablets. The calcium had done little to help because calcium by itself cannot do much. To be properly absorbed, calcium must be accompanied by magnesium, manganese, silica, boron, and phosphorous. Instead of calcium supplements, I put the women on a proper diet. In three months, the much needed minerals were replaced, and with that the osteoporosis disappeared.

## Lowered Immune Resistance

The link between sugar and lowered immune function is substantiated by hundreds of studies. Sugar can distort the chemistry of antibodies or reduce the effectiveness of lymphocyte cells. When you consume sugar every day, upwards of 50 percent of your antibody activity is neutralized for five hours, during which time the immune system cannot properly respond to all the millions of bacteria in the environment, and you become more vulnerable to infection.

## Aging

A recent critical study directly correlated high calorie intake from sugar with aging. For more than a decade, studies have shown that sugar speeds up the aging process by altering the way glucose attaches to proteins. This alteration can result in damaging cross-linkages in the protein molecules, which eventually causes stiffness and loss of elasticity.

To see sugar's effects, look at young people with wrinkled skin. Why would a forty- or fifty-year-old have wrinkles? Because they're smoking, drinking coffee and alcohol, and eating sugar. If you want to look younger, you don't have to visit the plastic surgeon; just eliminate sugar from your diet.

## Caffeine

Caffeine is so much a part of our lives that we cannot conceive of it as a dangerous substance. But if caffeine were invented today it would be banned as one of the more toxic drugs. Keep in mind, too, that most soft drinks, chocolate, and many over-the-counter pain relievers contain even more caffeine than coffee.

While caffeine acts as a mild stimulant to the central nervous system, offering a short-term sense of well-being and alertness, that feeling generally lasts only about five or ten minutes. Many people have bought into the falsehood that caffeine supplies us with continuous, harmless energy. That's simply not true, though it explains why many people need to drink many cups of coffee a day to feel "up."

The reality is that caffeine can cause heart palpitations, genetic damage, biological addiction, digestive disorders, cancer, and other serious ailments.

*Caffeine wires you.* If you already have a speeded-up metabolism and a challenged immune system, drinking caffeine means you're burning the candle at both ends.

*Caffeine is addictive.* Caffeine addiction is at the root of many caffeine-related disorders. Only recently have we been able to acknowledge that we can be addicted to substances other than drugs, such as caffeine and sugar. We know that caffeine is a common cause of insomnia and that in large doses it can be lethal.

Today we know that even in small quantities caffeine can cause problems. A single cup of coffee contains 30-100 mg of caffeine. A cappuccino boosts your intake to 300 mg. When you consider that a twelve-ounce can of cola has 50 mg of caffeine and look at the number of soft drinks consumed by children, an average child might get 250 mg of caffeine per day. We wonder, "Why can't they learn? Why can't they sit still in class?" Caffeine could be the culprit.

Rapid heartbeat, anxiety, gastrointestinal disturbances, indigestion, muscular twitches, insomnia, headache, and depression frequently take hold when the first dose of caffeine wears off. With larger doses, psychotic-like symptoms can manifest themselves. Caffeine wreaks havoc with the pancreas. Men should be aware that caffeine can have a deleterious affect on the prostate gland because it siphons off important minerals necessary to prostate health, such as zinc, and depletes the adrenal gland as well.

*Caffeine creates heart stress.* Caffeine can both stimulate and depress the blood vessels at the same time. It can elevate systolic and diastolic heartbeats causing an irregular rhythm. At John Hopkins University, the cardiovascular effects of caffeine were tested in male physicians over a period of twenty-five years. The results were dramatic. Those who drank three cups of coffee per day had twice as many coronary events as those who did not.

*Caffeine causes gastrointestinal distress.* Caffeine's disturbance to the gastrointestinal tract is less severe than to the heart, causing such minor conditions as indigestion and heartburn. More problematically, it destroys the enzymes in food. Therefore, when you drink coffee after a large meal, your body is deprived of the vital nutrients in food. Likewise, you should never take vitamins with caffeine.

*Caffeine causes genetic damage.* Caffeine has been proven to be dangerous to pregnant women because it affects genes and chromosomes and can harm a fetus. Caffeine can cause miscarriage, missing digits, cleft palate, and deformities of the skull. One study correlated an increased risk of fetal growth retardation with caffeine intake. This is not even controversial—it's a fact. When you drink coffee during pregnancy you're playing Russian roulette: You never know what the effect will be or which fetus it will affect.

Given the hard evidence, pregnant women should eliminate caffeine. Yet to date, the American Medical Association has done little, if anything, to alert the public to the dangers of caffeine. According to one analysis, researchers found that more than 70 percent (600 women) of the pregnant women in their sampling who drank caffeine during their first trimester—many of whom consumed 300 mg or more daily—miscarried.

## More Caffeine-Related Conditions

*Caffeine affects osteoporosis.* Caffeine weakens the bones by increasing the urinary calcium output. Caffeine washes calcium out of the system. Many women taking the required calcium and vitamin D supplements who also drink coffee daily found the supplements resulted in little improvement. One study showed that two cups of coffee a day will increase the risk of bone fracture.

*Caffeine exacerbates nervous system disorders.* Many clinicians see caffeine-induced over-stimulation of the nervous system, exacerbating problems in patients suffering from anxiety, depression, obsessive-compulsive disorder, and manic depression.

*Caffeine has been correlated with cancer.* Occurence of pancreatic cancer, which kills tens of thousands of Americans each year, has a strong statistical correlation with caffeine intake. A study performed at the Harvard School of Public Health concluded that two cups of coffee per day doubles the risk of developing pancreatic cancer.

### Alcohol

Social drinking has long been a way to bring people together. But, does it? Why do we need to drink alcohol with friends? Do we become more open and therefore closer? Or does alcohol actually keep us farther apart? Alcohol—and its dangers—has been completely misunderstood.

Alcohol presents a multitude of mental and physical health challenges. By changing the *ph* in your stomach it drains the body of vital folic acid, vitamin C, B-6, glutathione, and superoxide dismutase, all crucial to the health of the liver, kidneys, brain, and digestive system. Alcohol depresses the central nervous system, making us relaxed at first, then elated, but eventually it leads to depression. All the alcohol you consume creates free radicals which damage tissue, making you more susceptible to disease. Even normal, casual drinking is equivalent in free radical damage to smoking two packs of cigarettes. Alcohol adversely affects the pancreas and makes you more susceptible to diabetes and hypoglycemia. We haven't even mentioned cirrhosis of the liver.

### WINE

There has been much talk about the heart benefits of drinking wine, much of which is unfounded. The study that many people cite and assume to be conclusive attempted to show that drinking wine daily decreased the risk of heart disease. However, this was an epidemiological study which is an overview, not a real test where participants are followed for a period of time. What the wine does do is to flood the body with pro-antistatins that lower blood pressure and bad cholesterol (LDL) and raise good cholesterol (HDL) to help prevent arteriosclerosis. Pro-antistatins also have anticancer properties. Found in grape skin and grape seed, pro-antistatins are fifty times more powerful than vitamin E and twenty times more powerful than vitamin C as antioxidants; they also cause vitamin C to recycle throughout the body longer than it normally would. It's the ultimate anti-oxidant.

## Meat

Consuming meat today is truly hazardous. With the introduction of large-scale industrial farms, animals are being raised under crowded, dirty, and germ-infested conditions. Market demand necessitates pumping the animals with more chemicals and antibiotics than ever before. All meats today—beef, pork, and poultry—are laden with antibiotics. In the massive operation of taking meats from different sources and processing them together in huge plants, E-coli has entered our beef supply. And, with the introduction of feeding dead animals to live animals—science fiction come to life—new diseases are emerging. In Europe, this practice is believed to be the cause of Mad Cow Disease, which has killed many citizens.

In addition to these added toxins, red meat contains high levels of fat that congest the arteries. Cancer of the colon and the breast are also highly associated with the consumption of animal fat. It's not exactly known how the fat affects cancer growth; the fat itself may either be the cause of the cancer or it may allow some environmental substance to penetrate the body more easily.

## Dairy

Dairy products can present a multitude of problems to the heart, intestines, and immune system. Cheeses are high in fat, leading to hardening of the arteries. Cheese also contains casein, a coagulator that gives cheese its rubbery quality. Consider what that "glue effect" is doing in your body. Milk can also cause many deleterious effects because the antibiotics and synthetic hormones that are fed to cows also find their way into your body. In adults, milk is a common cause of intestinal disorders resulting from allergies or malabsorption problems. Cutting back milk does not mean losing valuable calcium; many foods, including seaweed, green vegetables, and a good supplement will supply your body with all the calcium you need.

It may take a little bit of time to rid ourselves of all of these unhealthy food products. But when we do, we're on our way toward preventing disease as well as reversing the aging of the cells. We're going to stay youthful and healthy.

### *Protecting Our Immune System*

In reality, we are as healthy as we choose to be. When I ask people how healthy they want to be, they look at me in amazement. A man might say, "What are you talking about? I'm a forty-year-old man, I have arthritis, gray hair, constipation, and fatigue. I don't have any choice in this. If I did, I would have done something about it a long time ago." But he can change. It's never too late—all it requires is that he make the choice to be healthy.

Recently, at a health support group, I asked the class what was happening in their lives since our last meeting. One woman, a schoolteacher, stood up and said, "You know, Gary, I was raised to believe in three square meals a day. I trusted that. Then I came to your class and found out that everything—*everything*—I've been eating is bad for me. Once I began to see that what you said made sense, I changed my habits. The first thing I noticed after the change was that the colds I would normally pick up from my students, which would ordinarily last for weeks,

30

only lasted a few days! I was getting better-quality sleep. If you can imagine the difference between waking up six or seven times and not waking up once, you'll know how powerfully this program has changed my quality of life."

I explained how her immune system had become stronger. When your immune system is working well you're not going to be susceptible to chronic problems. Many factors affect our immune system.

## Antibiotics

Today, we're taking more prescription and nonprescription drugs than ever before. Topping the list are antibiotics. In the 1940s, when they were first discovered, antibiotics were considered miracle cures. They wiped out such terminal diseases as scarlet fever, syphilis, and typhoid, and saved lives by stopping many diseases in their tracks. Soon doctors began prescribing antibiotics for everything, regardless of the type of microorganism causing the problem. The profusion of natural and semi-synthetic antibiotics caused almost boundless optimism.

Early on, though, it was clear that antibiotics worked only for some diseases and not others; more powerful strains of bacteria had developed that did not surrender to the drugs. In 1942, Sir Alexander Fleming, who discovered penicillin, warned physicians to use it with care due to the development of these antibiotic-resistant pathogens. But organized medicine chose not to heed these warnings, even going so far as to use penicillin prophylactically. During the disco craze, and later in the pre-AIDS era, people were taking megadoses of penicillin as a preventative measure against hepatitis B and what we now know as AIDS. That certainly didn't help.

31

Now, fifty or sixty years later, antibiotics have weakened our immune systems and caused yeast and microbes to build up in our digestive tracts. Antibiotics are also being used unnecessarily for conditions such as the common cold and flu, which are viral in nature. Antibiotics only affect bacterial problems.

When we truly need medications, we should take them judiciously. But we must make sure not to overuse them.

Antibiotics can harm the immune system in three different ways:

1. They suppress it by impairing the phagocytes and white blood cells, our main cellular defenders.
2. Antibiotics in the food you eat or taken directly multiplies and spreads *candida albicans,* challenging the digestive, nervous, and endocrine systems.
3. The antibiotics given to farm animals are transmitted to us through meat, chicken, and milk, causing tremendous overgrowth of microbes. This can cause over-sensitization to prescription antibiotics and possible allergic reactions.

### Laxatives

Bowel function is an uncomfortable subject for most people to discuss. As a result, we're uninformed about its great importance to our health. If you ask people how long it should take for food to be properly digested and evacuated from the body, they're clueless. Physicians don't even know the right answer; they typically say it could take a few days or a week, suggesting it's no big deal. In fact, it's quite a big deal. If our bodies evacuated at that rate we'd all be suffering from autotoxemia, an accumulation of bacteria that results in toxic bowels.

Bowels consist of one-third bacteria, and 90 percent of what remains is undigested cellulose and material that isn't assimilated into the body, as well as dead cells. This is all lethal material, and it's unhealthy to keep it in your body. Ideally, you should vacate with every meal. If not, you should evacuate approximately thirteen to twenty-four hours after eating, maximum.

The American diet is high in fat and protein, which is loaded with toxic nitrosamine, which slows down the intestines. Therefore, the longer those toxins remain in contact with the intestinal walls, the greater the risk of chemical reactions that can cause cancer. Coffee also destoys our ability to evacuate by removing important fluids from the bowels, causing them to become impacted. Colorectal cancer is now one of the leading causes of death, and it's completely preventable; it's not genetic, as many scientists insist.

We're now blaming everything on genes. The assumption is, if it's in our genes, it's certainly out of our hands. We're denying the plain and simple fact that we do have control over most of our health. In the case of our bowels, it is the lack of adequate fiber and liquids in our diet that can cause many of the diseases that are now misguidedly being ascribed to genetics.

Instead of changing our diet so that we eliminate the fat and caffeine, we pop laxatives. According to the American Society of Pharmacists, laxatives are the most widely misused class of drugs. I remember appearing on ABC television years ago, arguing about fiber with one of the top doctors in the AMA. He said, "Fiber is worthless. It's only good for pigs and cows." That's what the belief was at the time. Also, no one believed then that food or vitamins had anything to do with preventing disease, let alone treating it—outside of gross malnutrition.

## Mercury Dental Fillings

Mercury is highly toxic. It crosses the blood-brain barrier, attacks the nervous system, sets off allergens, and causes depression. Virtually every part of the body is susceptible to methyl mercury.

The dental establishment says that mercury amalgams in fillings are not toxic since they become inert several days after a filling has been placed. Not true. Throughout the day some of the mercury in your fillings is released. When this was first suggested many critics said, "There's no proof that the mercury is released." Today, we have that proof. Highly sensitized equipment now exists to detect the leaching of mercury every time you chew, drink a cold or hot beverage, or salivate. According to the Toxic Element Research Foundation, poisoning from mercury amalgams is one of the more serious health hazards facing us today.

## *It's in the Air*

Before we can make any kind of change we have to understand not just the foods and medications we take, but the world that surrounds us—the environment. Occasionally we'll read in the paper about some pollutant that has been unleashed, then quickly return to the sports pages, at great cost to our health.

## Environmental Pollutants

Air pollution is everywhere and affects us all. But

somehow people have difficulty understanding how bad the air is. Asbestos and fiberglass insulation materials that were once used in home construction, though banned now, are still in the atmosphere. We haven't cleaned all the buildings of asbestos; it's only removed when it's been detected. Urban air is filled with arsenic, copper, chromium, lead, cobalt, nickel, and silicon. People who work with heavy metals are particularly vulnerable to these toxins. A California Department of Health service report following companies that used lead showed that 97 percent of those companies have never monitored the amount of lead their employees have been exposed to. Yet the law requires them to do so.

## Indoor Air Pollution

What good does it do to have a good diet, to exercise, and then live in an environment that's polluted? A government study found that air pollution was ten times worse indoors than outdoors. Indoor pollution consists of carbon monoxide, nitrous oxides, and harmful particulates created by the combustion process in appliances, including gas stoves, water heaters, space heaters, and garages near living areas. When carbon monoxide is inhaled it binds with hemoglobin in the blood, blocking the flow of oxygen to the cells. At low doses, carbon monoxide can lower stamina, impair coordination, and adversely affect the immune system.

Another dangerous pollutant that infiltrates our homes is radon, a colorless, odorless gas that leaches from uranium deposits in the ground. When it disperses, radon is harmless, but when it's trapped in such closed spaces as a home or basement, it accumulates to unsafe levels and then decays into elements that can cause cancer. People who live in radon-rich areas of the country are exposed to levels the equivalent of 500 chest X-rays.

To the above pollutants add the wide variety of chemicals in our homes, such as formaldehyde (cleaning fluids), pressed wood which contains toxic adhesives (shelves, cabinets), benzene (inks, oils, and detergents), and the most dangerous of all, pesticides. In the office we're exposed to such dangers as electromagnetic pulses from computers, copiers, and cellular telephones. It's controversial, but there is evidence from groups of independent scientists that indicates that exposure to cellular phones (which emit a high level of heat)for more than two minutes per week can cause chromosomal damage to the brain.

The chemicals we so casually spew into the atmosphere damage the ozone layer that protects us from the sun's ultraviolet rays. As a result we're more vulnerable to skin cancer, and our crops and aquatic life are damaged.

### Water Pollution

Never drink tap water. Fluoride, which is added to our drinking water, is a known carcinogen. Mutagen, an immune depressant, and chlorine, a known cancer-causing agent, are also added to the water. Tap water also contains parasites that have not been filtered out. What's worse is that chlorine will not destroy the thousands of industrial chemicals and viruses in the water. Nor do our filtration systems remove microbes from the water.

Fluoride is a particularly toxic substance. Though we've been told it protects our teeth, this has not been proven. Scientists point to many studies that connect fluoride to serious health problems, including skin eruptions, collagen breakdown, headaches, gastric distress, immune system weaknesses, reproductive problems, genetic damage, kidney disease, hip fractures in the elderly, heart problems, and cancer. Considering the widespread use of fluoride, the implications are enormous. Fluoride is also added to our toothpaste. Yet, studies that have been conducted in communities where there is no fluoridation in the water supply show that there is no statistical difference in tooth decay there than in fluoridated areas. Proper dental hygiene protects us from decay.

We can do something about our environmental pollutants:

1. *Environmental and indoor air pollution*: Good air filters are available that will remove some of the toxins discussed. A strong filter can clear 25,000 cubic feet, an average- size house. These machines can remove virtually all the pollutants, including carbon monoxide, dander, molds, mildew, and particulates. You can create venting systems in your garage to draw toxic gases outside. You can do the same with radon by purchasing radon exhausts that will remove this gas from your living area.

2. *Water*: We can distill our water; we can filter it; we can buy water that has been cleansed of all chemicals. By doing so, at least we can make sure our number one nutrient is healthful.

Now that we've eliminated some of the major culprits that can compromise our body's natural defenses, we'll take the next step, which is to cleanse our body of toxins that are already there.

# Step #3:

## Cleansing and Detoxifying for Strength and Stamina

As we've seen, your body's ability to remain young and healthy is compromised by choosing nutrition-depleting foods. The good news is that you can do something to reverse that process. You can cleanse and detoxify your body by following the program outlined below. Cleansing the system requires that you identify the toxins that can, by themselves or in combination with other harmful ingredients, challenge the immune system and cause symptoms of premature aging. We'll go step by step, first identifying what you can do to rid your body of toxins and then moving towards rejuvenation. The cleansing process will involve the intake of liquids, juices, nutrients, herbs, and vitamins.

## *Cleanse Your Intestines*

When you detoxify what you are actually doing is assisting your body in its natural elimination processes. The initial area to cleanse is the intestines. Because of all the toxins in our food supply and because of a lack of wholesome, healthy, fibrous foods in our diet, we congest our intestines, making it almost impossible to absorb the nutrients we require from our food. This condition is called autotoxemia. When food is not properly absorbed it becomes a danger to the body. Further, when we take in fat, that fat slows down intestinal movement causing chronic constipation, which can lead to diverticulitis and other conditions of malabsorption.

> *Always remember, what we're working on here is wellness, not disease. We want to increase our energy, vitality, and our ability to rejuvenate.*

The first thing we can do to reverse this situation is to take in more liquid—at least one gallon a day. Start with clean, either filtered or bottled water in divided doses, drunk throughout the day. This helps to rehydrate the body and get everything moving inside. Ideally, your body should be 74 percent water. Most people, when measured by an impedance test, are only 68 percent water.

For each 1 percent below the ideal number, your energy level is reduced by 5 percent. When you don't have adequate water, your joints aren't properly lubricated and they become stiff and painful. When you drink enough water, you rid yourself of many ills, including constipation, arthritic pain, swelling and inflammation, localized pain, and musculoskeletal conditions; even migraine headaches decrease in frequency and severity.

It's not easy to drink the quantity of water I'm prescribing for cleansing. You'll have to adjust. But it's worth it.

Interestingly, senior citizens—who need it most—have the most problems drinking proper quantities of fluid. They complain of not feeling thirsty. As we age, the part of our brain that tells us when we're thirsty frequently becomes, like other systems, inefficient.

But thirst has nothing to do with it. Do not base your liquid requirements upon thirst. The first sign of not having enough water is fatigue. We can actually be severely dehydrated—causing weakness—and not know that it's because we haven't been drinking enough. Often when you exercise, you begin to feel run-down. The reason for this is water loss through sweating. Once you have a good drink, notice how you perk up again.

Water is being used here not to purify the system but to hydrate it and allow the biochemical functions to be more efficient. The next step, drinking juices, promotes purification.

## Juices

Three types of juices—vegetable, fruit, and herbal—are needed by the body for their vitamins, nutrients, and their detoxifying capabilities. You can prepare any combination of these that your body can tolerate. No two people's systems will handle the same juices in the same way.

Begin your juice program with 12-16 ounces of one vegetable juice each day. Always dilute the juice with 75 percent water. Celery and cucumber juice are particularly easy to tolerate and are very good at cleansing the system. They're not overly concentrated and have a natural diuretic action that helps people who are overweight or who suffer from edema. Others that are excellent as juice are dark green vegetables such as watercress, kale, parsley, dandelion greens, and arugula. Restrict yourself to one ounce—one ounce with 75 percent water—of these because they're highly concentrated. The chlorophyll and phytochemicals in the green vegetables cleanse the cells, and chelate (draw out) metals such as lead, cadmium, mercury, and aluminum. Chlorophyll also purifies the blood, which will help avoid problems with your liver and kidneys.

The liver is the septic system of the body, so you always want to keep it cleansed. The lymphatic system flushes viruses, bacteria, and cancer cells out of the body; it's important to keep that system clean as well. When people who have AIDS, breast cancer, and other lymphatic infections take these chlorophyll-rich juices into their bodies daily, the swelling in the lymph glands goes down.

Add to this combination a little bit of aloe vera. Don't juice aloe vera yourself, because the plant can contain bacteria. Buy an aloe vera that is easy on digestion from the health food store. Experiment with different brands to see which is most compatible with your system. Aloe is the number-one cleansing and detoxifying herb, and has been regarded as a miracle herb for thousands of years. It consists primarily of water, but the rest is essential oils, enzymes, phytochemicals (cancer fighters which occur naturally in plants), and healing polysaccharides. Aloe used in juice provides a multitude of healing agents that can rejuvenate damaged tissues. Think of all the damaged cells in your body, the damage in your arteries, the microlesions that can cause arteriosclerosis, and the debris-filled pockets in your intestines. Aloe stabilizes glucose and is good for diabetics and hypoglycemics. It has antibacterial, anti-inflammatory, and antiviral properties. It's a good natural laxative, terrific for ulcers, an immune booster, and it's easy to tolerate. Start by having one ounce of aloe juice mixed into 12 to 16 ounces of vegetable or fruit juice. Take it every day. It's one of the most important cleansing agents you can use.

Each month, add one more juice to your daily intake. In month-one of your cleansing program you'll have one vegetable juice per day; month-two, two juices; and month-three, three, and so on. Do this until you're drinking six juices per day. Bring in the fruit juices by month, too.

> *You don't have to prepare fresh juice every day. Adding lemon or vitamin C to the juice will keep it fully nutritious for 24 hours, and it can be kept refrigerated for two days.*

## *Getting Serious*

You're now getting the debris out of your intestines: with water first, and then juice. If you've been really mistreating your body by eating sugar, or you have some disturbance in your system such as cancer or candida, you'll want to detoxify in the second month, not the first. In this case, begin by taking one 12-ounce glass per day of grapefruits, lemons, limes, oranges, and star fruit. These provide specific phytochemicals—caprillic acid, a seed found in these fruits that produces a bitter oil—which kills hundreds of different pathogens and bacteria. Drink small quantities throughout the day to avoid diarrhea: four ounces every four hours or so.

## *Cleanse Your Body's Filtration System*

Since the liver filters toxins from the blood, it's important to keep it as clean as possible. To help flush out the liver, the best juices are purple cabbage, watermelon (the red flesh and the seeds are twice as nutritious as sunflower seeds), and black and red grapes, which have pro-antistatins (see Step 2 for more information), which are fifty times more powerful than vitamin E and twenty times more powerful than vitamin C as antioxidants. We don't want to rush this liver-flushing process. When you detoxify too fast, you end up with a healing crisis and overwhelm the body with dead cells.

The fruit juices, especially the red ones, are the great cleansers of the liver, particularly watermelon, cherries, pomegranate, cranberries, pink grapefruit, blood oranges, mangoes, and papaya. The phytochemicals in these are known to repair damage to the DNA. Hair grows back, gray hair returns to its original color, skin changes as pores become unclogged, vision improves, nails become stronger, digestion is more regular, and you even need less sleep. All of these good things result just from drinking juices.

## Reversing Damage

Let's say that when you were eighteen you spent the summer in the sun and received a couple of bad sunburns. The damage done from those burns is permanent because it changes your DNA. Every time you produce a new cell—you produce new skin approximately every ten months—that cell comes from damaged DNA. That's why our skin looks older as we age.

Much research is being done to discover how to repair DNA in such diseases as Parkinson's, Alzheimer's, and breast cancer. Researchers are about five years away from such discoveries, which is great, if the solutions are nontoxic.

In the meantime there is a natural way of reversing damage to DNA. The agent that does the job of reversing DNA damage is not vitamins, minerals, trace elements, or proteins or carbohydrates; it's phytochemicals. Not the green ones, but the red. The more we flood the body with healing phytochemicals, the quicker and the more complete the repair to the damaged DNA. Now the cell can do what it was meant to do, and we now have

47

a young cell again. In effect, we've rejuvenated ourselves.

After four years on this program, one forty-year-old man (who was closer to seventy biologically) transformed his biochemistry so that it was down into its thirties.

The whole principle behind the cleansing and detoxification in this program is rejuvenation. But don't stop and re-pollute yourself! Be consistent. Don't turn back. Just go forward.

## Fiber

Juices are approximately 60 percent of the whole cleansing process. The rest of the program is about making sure that the food you eat is high in fiber to cleanse the intestines.

To aid that process, every day for one month take non-dairy acidophilus. It's best taken in liquid form so you can get millions of live, healthy bacteria to replace the bad bacteria in your intestines. These are all residues from the days when you were eating sugar and other foods that fed bad bacteria. With acidophilus, you'll be getting 50 grams of fiber daily. After the first month, you can take the acidophilus every third day.

## Herbs

Now that you're cleansing your intestines with 50 grams of fiber daily, you'll also get that 50 grams by eating berries, such hot cereals as oatmeal, millet, buckwheat, or rice cereal, stir-fried or steamed vegetables, grains, and beans. Next, we want to make sure you're taking the right herbs. These are general guidelines. A skilled herbalist can help guide your selection and determine how much of an herb to use, when to use it, and in what form. As with all supplements, always check with your physician to determine which herbs might be counter-indicated with medicines you are currently taking, and, if you are pregnant.

### ALOE

A cleansing herb; in addition to its benefits to the colon, aloe can eliminate headache, irritability, and stabbing pain associated with menstrual cramps. Take one ounce aloe vera daily.

### ASTRAGULUS

A strenghtening herb; good for any defect in the immune system. Try taking 100 mg for one week and see how your body responds.

### B PROPELLUS

Anti-inflammatory, antibacterial, antioxidant. It's powerful for the flu, protects your heart, and can be used as a poultice. Check label for dosage.

### BILBERRY

Promotes and enhances cleansing and detoxification; also improves the microvascular system. It is also recommended for prevention of macular degeneration. Check label for dosage.

### CRANBERRIES

Great for the bladder, particularly when infected. Also lowers blood pressure. Include in your daily diet.

### DANDELION

Rich in potassium, dandelion is a good diuretic since it doesn't leach potassium from the body as do other diurectics. A great liver detoxifier and full of vitamin A. Add dandelion leaves to your salads or put them in your juicer every day for a rich tonic.

### ECHINACEA

An immune enhancer, a liver detoxifier, and digestive tonic, good for warding off colds and the flu in their early stages. Take 100 mg daily for one week per month; prolonged use decreases its efficacy.

### FLAXSEED OIL

Contains the essential fatty acid Omega-3 which nourishes the brain; it also has anticancer properties, particularly for colon and breast cancer. Take 1 tablespoon daily.

### GARLIC

One of the most popular herbs for cleansing and detoxifying. Helps the intestine, lowers blood pressure, lowers cholesterol, stimulates the immune system, and fights viruses. Take 1,000 mg of garlic daily.

### GINSENG

Probably the most researched herb in the world, ginseng contains germanium which pulls mercury and excess hydrogen from the cells, giving the body a higher proportion of energy-boosting oxygen. It also helps the body stay in balance when under stress. Take 500 mg daily.

### HAWTHORN

Anyone over the age of forty-five should be drinking hawthorn. Used throughout Europe as a heart tonic, good for arterial and peripheral stimulation. Take 65 mg daily.

### MILK THISTLE

Another terrific liver detoxifier, milk thistle helps the liver process toxins and poisons. Take 125 mg daily.

### MOTHERWORT

Helps stabilize the electrical rhythm of the heart. Dosage should be monitored by your doctor.

### ROSEMARY

Highly researched, rosemary is even more highly recommended than soy for breast-protecting capabilities. Include in your daily diet.

### SAW PALMETTO

The standard herbal remedy for prostate problems. A sexual stimulant and energy booster for men. Take 30 mg daily.

### ST. JOHN'S WORT

An effective, mild, natural treatment for depression. Take 300 mg three times daily. Expect to wait two to three weeks before you feel the full effects.

### TURMERIC

Good anticancer herb. Turmeric contains a vital phytochemical that prevents mammary tumors in animals. Include in your daily diet.

*YOHIMBI*

An impotence fighter. Take 100 mg and observe label precautions.

*VALERIAN*

For anxiety, especially in women. Take 200 mg daily.


## Herb Teas

Herb teas are not only rich in nutritional benefits and curative effects, the quieting effect of drinking tea is calming in itself. Drinking tea can also satisfy your daily water consumption requirement.

*GREEN TEA*

Green tea, with its tiny supply of caffeine, is a nice alternative to coffee. It gives you a little lift without the negative side effects of coffee. It also has anti-cancer properties and is an effective immune system stimulator.

*RED CLOVER*

Rich in isoflavones and curcuminoids, red clover is a powerful fighter of hormone connected cancers, like breast and prostate cancer.

*STINGING NETTLE*

One of the most nutrient-rich substances available, loaded with carotenes and calcium. Stinging nettle is of benefit for benign prosthetic hypoplasia. It is also good for overall cleansing and detoxification

*Note*: There are other herbs for other conditions. We're concentrating here, however, on what goes into a cleansing program.

## Rejuvenation

The first and most important part of the revitalization process is eating a vegetarian diet. In a vegetarian diet you avoid meat, sugar, and processed carbohydrates, and replace animal protein with beans, grains, legumes, nuts, and seeds. You can have fish, but no other animal products. Much research and scientific literature is filled with good news about the vegetarian diet and its wide-ranging benefits. You'll want to add all the good vitamins, minerals, and nutrients listed below to jump-start your immune and other systems.

## Vitamins, Minerals, and Nutrients

Always check with your doctor before you begin a detoxification and rejuvenation program to make sure there are no counter-indications between the supplements you will be taking and any medicines you are on.

### ACETYL-L-CARNITINE
The single most powerful antioxidant for your brain, acetyl-L-carnitine crosses the blood-brain barrier. Taking between 500 and 1,500 mg daily can do wonders for mental function. Really good for senior citizens; keeps your mind working as it should.

### ALPHA-LIPOIC ACID

Another terrific antioxidant that protects cells against aging and disease and makes the mind more lucid. Take between 50 to 100 mg daily. It can increase insulin's working capacity, encouraging glucose disposal. It also helps with cataracts and strokes by incapacitating hydroxyl free radicals which result in damage to the eye from oxidative stress.

### ACIDOPHILUS

Great colon cancer preventative, it reestablishes healthy probiotic bacteria which counters destructive bacteria. Check label for dosage.

### ASCORBYL-PALMITATE

This lipid or fat-soluble type of vitamin C can work up to eight hours in your body. Most vitamin C is used up quickly, only staying in your body from a half-hour to one hour, depending upon the illness you have. Take 200 mg daily.

### BETA CAROTENE

A terrific source of vitamin A, beta carotene can be found in carrot juice and vegetables of a yellow-orange or dark green color. It bolsters the immune system, inhibits viruses, and prevents premature aging. It's also terrific for the eyes. Take 15,000 to 25,000 IU daily.

### BIOTIN

A member of the B-complex family, biotin keeps hair, skin, bone marrow, and glands healthy. Take 30 mcg daily.

### BORAGE-SEED OIL

Borage provides gamma-linolenic acid, a strong anti-oxidant; it also contains omega-3s. Take four to six 500 mg capsules daily.

### BORON

Boron can reverse the symptoms of osteoarthritis. You need take only 3 mg daily.

### CALCIUM (FROM CITRATE)

Calcium is the body's chief mineral and the principle component of bones and teeth. Calcium deficiency will show itself in nervousness, depression, headaches, and insomnia. Take 800 to 1,200 mg daily. Women at risk for osteoporosis should take a higher daily dosage.

### CHOLINE

Found in wheat germ and bran, beans, egg yolks, brewer's yeast, whole grain, nuts, lecithin, choline helps regulate cholesterol levels and is vital to the liver's functions. Choline aids in building and maintaining a healthy nervous system. Take 30 mcg daily.

### CHROMIUM

Chromium is important to the heart, liver, brain, and glucose metabolism system. It is vital to the production of protein and to white blood sells. It helps fight bacteria, viruses, toxins, arthritis, cancer, and premature aging. To counteract stress, the adrenal glands must have an adequate supply of chromium. Chromium can be found in whole wheat flour, all whole grain cereals, fresh fruit juices, legumes, and leafy vegetables. Take 50 to 200 mcg daily.

### CITRUS BIOFLAVONOIDS

Lemons, plums, and oranges, among other fruits are rich in bioflavonoids, which help prevent cancer, aid in the healing of bruises, and counteract capillary fragility. Bioflavinoids also help your body utilize vitamin C. Take 300 mg daily.

### COENZYME Q10

This is a superstar. Coenzyme helps prevent heart attacks and strokes by increasing the oxygenation of the mitochondria, which supplies energy to heart cells. As an antioxidant, it prevents the damage to blood vessels which leads to hardening of the arteries. Take 50 and 150 milligrams for mild heart disease.

### CONJUGATED LINOLENIC ACID (CLA)

A wonderful immune booster. Good for people with multiple sclerosis; has anticancer properties; lowers bad cholesterol (LDL) and triglycerides. Take 500 mg daily.

### DHEA

Produced by the adrenal glands, this is the key hormone associated with aging. Before taking DHEA you should be tested to see if you have a deficiency. If you do not, it should not be used as a supplement. Take 10 to 25 mg daily.

### FOLIC ACID

Folic acid works mostly in the brain and nervous system. It is a vital component of spinal and extra-cellular fluid. It is necessary for the manufacture of RNA and DNA. Take 400 mcg daily.

### GLUTATHIONE (REDUCED)

Made up of three amino acids—glytamic, glycine, and cystine—this does everything: reduces cholesterol, stimulates the immune system; reduces fat; and benefits those with arthritis, diabetes, and heart disease. Take 200 mg daily.

### INOSITOL

Inositol is responsible for breaking down fats. It plays role in preventing cholesterol buildup and normalizing fat metabolism. Studies indicate that inositol has an anxiety-reducing effect similar to some tranquilizers. Insomnia, hair loss, high cholesterol levels, or cirrhosis of the liver may indicate a deficiency of inositol. Take 500 milligrams daily.

### IODINE

Iodine, which is found in blue-green algae, sunflower seeds, kelp, and sea salt, is one of the building blocks of great skin. It helps heal infections, increases oxygen consumption, and helps prevent skin roughness and premature wrinkling. Take in small amounts.

### LYCOPENE

Found in red fruits, lycopene is a powerful liver detoxifier; it is also a cancer fighter and has been correlated specifically with the prevention of prostate cancer. Take 250 mg daily.

### MAGNESIUM (FROM CITRATE)

Found in dark, leafy vegetables, and whole grains, magnesium calms the nerves. A lack of magnesium is also associated with eating disorders such as indigestion, flatulence, abdominal pain, cramps, and constipation. Take 1,500 mg daily.

## MELATONIN

Melatonin is a brain hormone released by the pineal gland, and it diminishes with age. Taken at bedtime it can help normalize sleep, and protect your brain from free radical damage. This is one of the best antioxidants for the brain. Take one to 3 mgs daily.

## MOLYBDENUM

Important trace element that may help fight cancer. Take 100 mcg daily.

## NAC

A proven cancer fighter, NAC improves the immune system, and fights heart disease. Take 500 mg daily.

## OLIVE OIL

This should be the oil in your daily diet. A great healing nutrient, olive oil is rich in essential fatty acids.

## OMEGA FATTY ACIDS

Omega-3s, 6s, and 9s are found in essential fatty acids, and are needed for the breakup of cholesterol, the transportation of fat, and the regulation of hormones. They promote weight loss, boost immunity, heal skin conditions, and even help prevent breast and prostate cancer. Flaxseed oil, extra-virgin olive oil, sesame and pumpkin oils are all excellent sources of omega oil, as is fatty fish. In supplement form take between four and six 500 mg capsules of primrose or borage oil daily.

### PARA-AMINOBENZOIC ACID (PABA)

Eggs, brewer's yeast, molasses, wheat germ, and whole grains are a good source of PABA. Paba acts as a coenzyme in the metabolism of proteins. It helps manufacture healthy blood cells and is excellent for healing skin disorders, and as a sun shield. Take 400 to 600 iu daily.

### PANTOTHENIC ACID (VITAMIN B5)

An important B-complex vitamin that will supercharge your adrenal glands. Along with vitamin C, it counteracts the toxic effects of sugar and caffeine. Take 5 mg daily.

### PHOSPHATIDYL SERINE

A crucial element within your brain cell membrane, it has direct anti-aging effects on your brain, offering much promise for Alzheimer's and Parkinson's diseases. Take 500 mg daily.

### POTASSIUM

In conjunction with sodium, potassium helps form an electrical pump that speeds nutrients into every cell of the body. It is particularly vital to the digestive and endocrine systems, muscles, brains, and nerves. Leafy green vegetables, bananas, cantaloupes, avocados, dates, and prunes are good sources of potassium. Take 500 mg daily.

### QUERCETIN

An anticancer bioflavonoid. Take 200 to 800 mg daily.

### SAMe

A nontoxic, natural amino acid found in all bodily tissues and necessary for proper utilization of melatonin. It alleviates, among other ills, arthritis and depression. Take 200 mg daily. Check with your physician if you are taking any other anti-depressants.

### SELENIUM

A trace element found in fish, wheat germ, and garlic, useful in the prevention and treatment of cancer, it has anti-aging properties as well. Take 50 to 200 mcg daily in the pill form.

### SUPEROXIDE DISMUTASE

An important antienzyme nutrient produced by the body. It is not effective when taken orally unless it is enteric-coated. Manganese and copper, together with zinc, support the action of superoxide dismutase.

### VITAMIN B COMPLEX

The B complex vitamin plays an important role in maintaining healthy metabolism, and in activating our enzymatic system, converting glucose and fatty acids into energy. It also helps the adrenal glands control how fat is deposited in the body. Take 50 mg daily.

### VITAMIN B-1 (THIAMINE)

Vitamin B-1 is essential to normal metabolism and nerve function. It is found in a variety of foods, including whole grains, legumes, poultry, and fish. Take 1 to 1.5 mg daily.

### VITAMIN B-2 (RIBOFLAVIN)

Found in dairy products, meat, poultry, fish, nutritional yeast, whole grains and leafy vegetables, B-2 helps promote rapid growth and repair of tissues, and enhances a cell's ability to exchange gases, such as oxygen and carbon dioxide, in the blood. It helps release energy from food and is essential for good digestion. Take 1.4 mg daily.

### VITAMIN B-6 (PYROXIDINE)

Vitamin B-6 nourishes the central nervous system, controls sodium-potassium levels in the blood, and assists in the production of red blood cells and hemoglobin. B-6 is found in many foods including eggs, peanuts, whole grains, beans, and organ meats. Along with B-2 it helps promote the proper growth and repair of tissues. Take 5 mg daily.

### VITAMIN B-12 (COBALAMIN)

Vitamin B-12 aids in the metabolism of all proteins and amino acids and cell reactions called methylation. Fermented foods, such as tofu or tempeh, and poultry and meat are rich in B-12. Take 2.4 mcg daily. If you are a vegetarian, you should include a low-potency vitamin supplement with your diet.

### VITAMIN C

Vitamin C strengthens the immune system, keeps cholesterol levels down, combats stress, promotes fertility, protects against cardiovascular disease and various forms of cancer, maintains mental health, and ultimately may prolong life. Oranges and other citrus fruits, sprouts, berries, tomatoes, sweet potatoes, and green leafy vegetables are important sources of vitamin C. Symptoms of deficiency include bleeding gums, a tendency to bruise easily, shortness of breath, and lowered resistance to infection. Take—in water-soluble form—anywhere from a low of 90 mg to a high of 2,000 mg daily.

*VITAMIN D-3*

Vitamin D helps the body utilize calcium and phosphorus to form strong bones and teeth, and healthy skin. Its action is also vital to the nervous system. A prime source of vitamin D is sunshine, but its preferable to get it from food sources, such as milk, butter, egg yolks, sardines, salmon, tuna and fish liver oils. Signs of deficiency include brittle and fragile bones, pale skin, and irregular heartbeats. Take 5 to 10 mcg daily.

*VITAMIN E*

Vitamin E is basically an antioxidant; it protects our fatty acids from destruction and maintains cellular health and integrity. Vitamin E is also an excellent first-aid tonic for burns. Wheat germ and wheat germ oil, leafy plant foods, whole grains, and nuts are good sources of vitamin E. Take anywhere from 400 to 1,000 IU daily.

### *Maintain Great—but Realistic—Expectations*

As with any kind of change, you must be patient with yourself and with the process. Give yourself time to reverse the poor health habits and premature aging to which your body has been subjected. Under ideal circumstances, it's going to take two to five years for you to see real change. You'll notice some improvements, however, much sooner than that. Within two to three weeks, you'll require less sleep, have a better sense of well-being, fewer aches and pains, more energy than you had before, and you'll sleep through the night. Things that you have taken for granted will improve, too: Your nails will get stronger; your hair and skin will shine.

It is important to note that when you start a cleansing and detoxification program, you will generally go through one to two weeks of feeling worse before you feel better. Your skin may break out, you may see bacterial discharge in discoloration of mucous, notice new body odors, and you may require extra sleep. All of these are signs that your body is releasing toxins. Let it happen. Let the process do its work. When you stop taking in processed foods and replace them with a vegetarian diet, following the above regimen, and the other six steps in this program, you will begin to rid your body of toxins that have been there for years. All processed foods contain harmful pesticides, hormones, pollutants, and sugars. Detoxifying frees up the enzymes in your body so they can do the job that they were meant to do: keep you young, vital, and healthy.

The real total cleansing and reversal of your body chemistry—the ground-up restoration—is going to take years. I can't say this enough: Be patient. Stay away from any miracle cures. There is no magic shortcut here. Everything you're doing is based on good scientific testing and principles. When you stay with this program, you'll experience all the benefits you're hoping for.

## Step #4:

### Eating Well Is the Best Revenge

Once you've brought whole grains, beans, lots of fruits and vegetables, and the vegetarian foods described in this step into your diet, supermarket shopping will never be the same. You're traveling down new aisles now. You won't miss those greasy hamburgers when you're enjoying the nutty, sweet, and exotic flavors of the best vegetarian cuisine.

## Great Grains

For anyone following a vegetarian diet, whole grains are versatile and rich in flavor, as well an essential staple. Organic grains contain all the right enzymes, phytochemicals, and complete proteins that your body requires. Varying the grains you eat will also vary the nutrients available to you. Grains are delicious and truly satisfying food. They can taste sweet or nutty, or be crunchy and chewy in texture. Everything goes with grains: beans, vegetables, fruits, nuts and seeds. And today, grains can be found everywhere—not only in health food stores, but in your supermarket as well.

## Cooking Grains

1. Rinse grains thoroughly. (On the surface of any grain are molds that cause allergic reactions, bacteria, fungi, and parasites. When you rinse grains, you wash off all of these substances.)
2. Bring 2 cups water to a boil.
3. Place 1 tablespoon macadamia oil—which tolerates heat well—into the pot of water to prevent grains from clumping.
4. Add 1 cup grains to *boiling* water. (Most people start cooking grains in cold water which tends to make them clump. Adding grains to boiling water yields a flakier grain.)
5. Bring to a second boil, cover, and simmer for anywhere from 10 to 45 minutes depending upon the grain.
6. Turn off the heat but leave the lid on for 20 minutes and serve.

For a crunchier texture and a sweeter flavor, try dry-roasting or sautéing grains before cooking.

- To dry roast, place grains in a cold cast-iron or steel skillet and toss in the pan until they pop and a nutty aroma emerges.

- To sauté, heat a skillet that is evenly coated with a small amount of oil. Do not let oil get too hot or it will smoke. Place grains in skillet and stir until a few kernels pop and a nutty aroma emerges.

> **NOTE:** *Most grains double in size from their raw to their cooked state. Therefore one cup of uncooked grains will yield two cups of cooked grain and feed two to three enthusiastic grain eaters or three to four as a side dish.*

## Amaranth

If you're allergic to wheat, amaranth is a great substitute. Sweet in flavor, the amaranth seed is tiny, like a grain of sand, but it is unusually high in protein which carries high levels of lysine, one of the most vital amino acids. It is also higher in iron and calcium than conventional grains.

It's also extremely versatile. For an Eastern flavor, add scallions, shiitake mushrooms, toasted sesame oil, miso, soy sauce, and turmeric.

For a sweet porridge, add blanched peanuts, roasted cashews, raisins, and cinnamon.

## Barley

Barley is a perhaps the oldest and certainly the most adaptable grain on the planet. Hull-less barley contains two or three times the protein of an equal portion of rice. It's known to lower cholesterol; some studies indicate the reduction is as much as 25 percent, which is more than most medications.

*Note:* Some people have allergic reactions to barley. Check with your doctor to determine if you are susceptible.

Unhulled barley is almost impossible to cook due to its hard outer shell. Most available barley is pearled, which lightens the color. But make sure it is not too pearled since pearling depletes it of nutrients; look for darker pearled barley instead.

Barley is also versatile and can be made into a variety of dishes like cold or hot breakfast cereal, hot mushroom barley soup, barley-nut mushroom casserole, and can be stuffed into cabbage or grape leaves. Barley is great for dieters: it's light, chewy, and filling.

### COOKING BARLEY

- Boiling: Use 2 1/2 cups liquid to 1 cup barley. Barley cooks for approximately thirty minutes: fifteen minutes of cooking at a boil and fifteen minutes at a low simmer. If too chewy, add another 1/2 cup water until it reaches the desired texture. For a sweeter taste, roast before cooking.
- Pressure cooking: use 2 cups water to 1 cup grain. Cook for 20 minutes.

## Buckwheat

Buckwheat is actually not a true grain but a grass seed related to rhubarb. Buckwheat can be bought as whole-roasted or unroasted, cut or uncut groats, or as roasted buckwheat flour, which makes terrific pancakes, waffles, and breads. Buckwheat is particularly high in thiamin, riboflavin, and other b-complex vitamins, with exceptional amounts of calcium, phosphorus, and other minerals. It also contains a high lysine content, greater than any other cereal.

### COOKING BUCKWHEAT

Buckwheat cooks quickly; you almost never have to bring it to a boil. You can even prepare buckwheat without cooking:

1. Toast 1 cup groats in a saucepan over medium-high heat for 3 to 4 minutes and gives off a deep nutty aroma.
2. Heat 2 cups water or vegetable stock (hot, not boiling).
3. Place buckwheat directly into heated water. Cover and let sit for 5 to 10 minutes and serve.

The result will have a porridge-like consistency. If you prefer more of a brown rice-style consistency, cook the buckwheat and adjust water and heat to preferred texture.

> **NOTE:** *The key to eating right is variety, which gives you everything you need for your well-being.*

---

BUCKWHEAT CREAM

1. Sauté 1 cup buckwheat flour in oil in a heavy skillet
2. Allow to cool and return to heat; gradually add the 2 cups water and bring to a boil.
3. Stir and simmer for ten minutes, or until it reaches the desired consistency.
4. Add any of your favorite spices and sweeteners: raw honey, rice syrup, or stevia. Adding allspice, cinnamon, anise, cloves, or fennel not only brings flavor to the cereal but is terrific for gastrointestinal disorders and killing off bacteria as powerful as E-coli.

---

## Soba Noodles

The Japanese soba noodle is made with buckwheat flour and makes a great substitute for wheat pasta. Cooked like a pasta—but more quickly—soba can be prepared with a multitude of sauces, including marinara with olives and garlic and onion. You can prepare soba as a stew.

---

SOBA STEW

1. Choose a selection of vegetables including burdock root, lotus root, and starchy vegetables, including squash, strong leafy vegetables like Chinese cabbage or Chinese celery.
2. Place in pot and cover with water.
3. Cook for thirty to forty-five minutes.
4. Add miso paste to taste.
5. When cooking is almost complete, add soba noodles and cook until tender but with a bite.

---

## Corn

I'm not a big advocate of corn since it's genetically engineered and processed with pesticides; though I do like organic corn, stone-ground corn flour, or corn-meal—which has been used as a staple for thousands of years. Yellow cornmeal contains about 10 percent protein and is higher in vitamin A than white corn. Sweet corn is usually steamed in water, while field corn is likely to be ground into meals and flours. (The difference between a meal and a flour is in its coarseness.) The germ of cornmeal begins deteriorating in a matter of hours, necessitating immediate use. Don't let it sit on the shelf.

### CORN BREADS

Cornmeal makes absolutely delicious and satisfying corn bread, southern spoon bread, johnnycakes, and muffins. They're all easy to prepare, and you can add raisins, fruits, nuts, and a variety of ingredients to enhance flavor, texture, and nutritional value.

---

### CREAMED CORN

*I love creamed corn. As a child I often ate it over stewed cabbage.*

1. Cut off the corn kernels down to where the milky fluid flows.
2. Place in pot with enough rice milk to cover.
3. Add a dash of salt and pepper.
4. Cook gently for five minutes.

---

## Millet

The most commonly eaten grain in Africa, millet has many virtues. Rich in alkaline, it is the most easily digested of all the grains, and one of the sweetest. It's an intestinal lubricant and has a well-balanced amino acid structure, providing a low-gluten protein. Millet is rich in calcium, lecithin, and riboflavin. Tasty with carrot sauce, tofu-dill mustard sauce, sweet and sour sauce, or any topping you would use with brown rice; millet also makes a delicious breakfast cereal prepared hot with fresh fruit, your preferred sweetener, cinnamon, rice milk, raw honey, and a spoonful of protein powder.

### If This Is Deprivation . . .

*Feeling deprived because you can't have breads made from whole wheat or white flour? Listen to this: grain flours are extraordinary in their range of flavors and uses. You can make everything your taste buds crave in breads, cookies, cakes, and muffins with a single or a combination of grain flours. Consider making tasty pancakes of brown rice flour and soy flour or buckwheat and barley flour. Each gives you a different taste and consistency. Don't be afraid to experiment. You'll be amazed and delighted by the great range of offerings. You call this deprivation? I'd call it a wealth of gustatory offerings.*

Millet also makes a satisfying stuffing. Add it to hollowed-out zucchini or mushroom caps. Millet meal or flour is a good grain to combine with other flours in bread as it adds calcium, protein, and lecithin.

### COOKING MILLET

Use the same method as with other grains. Allow only five minutes to cook. Millet expands in cooking more than any other grain—one cup of raw millet turns into four cups of cooked grain.

---

### SUPER-ENERGY BREAKFAST MILLET

*A morning that starts with this dish will keep you going for a good five hours—you won't even think of a midmorning snack. When you eat right, you're not always hungry!*

1. Cook one cup millet.
2. Blend walnuts, pecans, almonds, bananas, raspberries, peaches, and strawberries (in season) and rice milk.
3. Pour mixture over the millet and add a scoop of protein powder.

---

## Brown Rice

Rich in fiber, extremely low in sodium and fat, and cholesterol free, rice is composed almost 80 percent of complex carbohydrates with only a little protein, phosphorous, and potassium. Whole grain brown rice, unlike white rice, has not had its nutritious bran and endosperm removed. It's available in short, medium, long-grain, and sweet varieties. The differences are largely aesthetic. The shorter the grain, the more gluten, which means it cooks up stickier; long grain cooks up fluffier. Sweet rice grain is the most glutenous of all. It's excellent for cereals and rice balls.

### COOKING BROWN RICE

1. Bring 2 1/2 cups of water to a boil.
2. Place 1 tablespoon macadamia oil in boiling water.
3. Add 1 cup rice, bring to a boil, and let simmer for twenty-five minutes. Stir regularly to prevent bottom grains from sticking and scorching.

### PRESSURE-COOKED RICE

Short grain: 2 cups water to 1 cup grain
Medium grain: 1 1/2 cups water to 1 cup grain
Long grain: 1 1/4 cups water to 1 cup grain
When rice is cooked, allow the pressure to return slowly to normal. The cooling steam will add moisture to the grain helping it to cook to completion.

---

### BROWN RICE CREAM
1. Bring 4 cups lightly salted water to a boil.
2. Add 1 cup dry-roasted brown rice.
3. Cook for 5 minutes over low heat, stirring constantly to prevent lumping.
4. Add 1 cup rice milk, or puree one pint blueberries and pour the syrup into the rice porridge.

---

## SWEET RICE BALLS

*For your sweet tooth, take this to the movies instead of a chocolate bar. It tastes too good to be helping your heart, your lungs, your liver—your whole body—but it will.*

1. Prepare sweet rice (follow direction for cooking rice).
2. Combine 2 tablespoons almond butter, diced figs, dates, currants, and pine nuts, and shape into balls.
3. Place in refrigerator for one hour to firm.

### BROWN RICE FLAKES

Brown rice is also available in flake form. The flaking process was originally developed to improve animal nutrition and can help us as well. Add flakes to any dish, including soups or casseroles for richer texture and to boost protein content.

### KOKOH (RICE MILK)

A grain milk which has become very popular, rice milk looks like cow's milk and replaces whole milk in our diet. If your children like Ovaltine or chocolate in their milk, just stir it into rice milk instead. They'll love it. It looks, tastes, has the same consistency, and cooks up just like milk. You can make ice cream, yogurt and cheese from rice milk. It has no animal protein, no saturated fat, and no cholesterol. It's the easiest substitution you can make. Try a blindfold test replacing cheddar or Parmesan cheese made from cow's milk with rice milk. See if you can tell the difference. You can't.

## The Milk Allergy Test

*Rice milk is a lifesaver for anyone allergic to milk. If you suspect that your child's congestion and constant sinus infections are caused by a milk allergy, try this test. Empty the real milk carton and fill it with rice milk. Let your child make a chocolate drink with it and see if she can tell the difference. In a few days, see if your child's congestion, bedwetting, ear or eye infections disappear.*

## Triticale

Triticale is a highly nutritious grain, rich in protein (17 percent), and a good balance of all nutrients. Use as a whole grain in casseroles, use the flour in bread, and the flakes in granola. Triticale flour is especially good in breads with its nutty, sweet flavor and high-protein content. It's low in gluten and should be mixed with other more glutenous flours to hold firm.

## Bulgur

Bulgur is whole wheat berries that have been steamed and hulled, then dried and cracked. It is a staple in the Middle East and most commonly found in tabouli salad. Bulgur requires no cooking (see preparation directions below).

## TABOULI

*Preparing the bulgur:*
1. 1 cup bulgur, rinsed and placed in a stainless steel bowl.
2. Pour 1 cup of boiling water into bulgar, stir, and place a towel over the bowl.
3. Let sit for fifteen minutes during which time the bulgur will germinate, absorb all the water, and open up.

*Preparing the salad:*
   1 small, sweet onion, chopped
   1/2 cup raisins
   1 tablespoon olive oil
   1 teaspoon toasted sesame oil
   1 teaspoon tamari soy sauce (or to taste)
   1/4 cup sunflower seeds

1. In a blender, combine above ingredients to desired consistency, and mix with bulgur.
2. Serve chilled.

### Couscous

A soft, refined durham wheat flour or semolina that has been steamed, cracked, and dried, couscous can be prepared by adding 1 cup of grain to 2 cups of boiling water. Let sit until water is completely absorbed, approximately 3 minutes.

### Quinoa

A staple of the Inca Indians and known as the mother grain, quinoa is a complete protein. The germ, equivalent to the yolk of an egg, is the most power-packed part of any seed. Quinoa is closer to the ideal protein balance than any other grain, being at least equal to milk in protein quality. This dynamic grain is high in B vitamins, iron, zinc, potassium, calcium, and vitamin E.

Cook in normal grain ratios for ten to fifteen minutes. When cooked it will triple in quantity. It's a light grain with a delicate taste.

---

*NUTTY QUINOA*
1 cup cooked quinoa (at room temperature)
1/2 apple, cut into bite-size pieces
1/4 cup walnuts, chopped

Combine all ingredients, and serve immediately.

---

### Whole Wheat

Whole wheat still holds a prominent position among grains because of its versatility and high nutritional value. Containing anywhere from 6 to 20 percent protein, wheat is also a source of vitamin E and large amounts of nitrates.

### Oats

Research indicates that oats contain an alkaloid that apparantly enhances vitality, especially for men. Oats also help regulate blood sugar; they contain compounds that prevent cancer in animals, combat inflammation of the skin, and act as a laxative.

You can use oats in several different forms: steel cut, which are chewy; whole rolled oats; and Scotch or Irish oats. Soak overnight before cooking as a porridge. Oats can also be used as a flour.

> ## Grain Tips
>
> **You don't have to cook grains from scratch everyday. Grains will last for three days in the refrigerator.**

## Beans (Legumes)

Beans are an important, inexpensive source of complete protein equal to animal protein. Loaded with vitamins and minerals, they're also rich in phytochemicals, which can help rebalance hormones in the body—particularly good for women in menopause. Beans lower cholesterol, blood pressure, and tryglycerides. Beans are great cleansers of the intestinal tract. They can be eaten whole, flaked, or dried. There are over eighty varieties of beans.

### Cooking Beans

One cup of dried beans will make four servings, cooked. Adzuki, black, white, navy, chickpeas, soy, and white (kidney) beans should all be soaked overnight (does not apply to lentils). Soaking beans removes gas and other digestive problems.

As an alternative to soaking you can bring one cup of

beans and three cups of water to a boil. Remove pot from stove and cover. Let beans sit for an hour. Return the beans to the heat and bring to a boil. Allow to simmer for 20 minutes.

When cooking beans for soup, use five times as much water as beans. Do not salt the water until the beans are soft, since salt will draw moisture from the beans and make them dry.

*Bean Tips. Once you've cooked beans, they'll stay fresh in the refrigerator for a week. You can then use them in a variety of ways: hot or cold, or as a puree.*

### PUREED WHITE BEANS
1. *Add chopped raw garlic, chopped onions, tahini (sesame paste), and lemon juice to beans.*
2. *Puree in blender.*

### Adzuki beans

Adzuki are small red beans that are used in Japan both in cooking and for medicinal purposes as a remedy for kidney ailments. Very high in vitamin B and trace minerals, adzukis should never be pressure-cooked because it renders them bitter.

## Black beans

Black beans have served as a major food source in the Caribbean, Mexico, and the American Southwest for many years. They are as high in protein as steak, without the cholesterol. Black beans should never be pressure-cooked since their skins fall off easily and may clog the valve. A smooth, rich black bean soup, a specialty of Cuba, is made by cooking the soaked beans until tender, adding sautéd garlic, onions, and celery, and then pressing the mixture through a colander.

## Black-Eyed Peas

A southern favorite. Provides a delicious, complete protein-balanced meal. Among the quickest cooking beans, they become tender in 45 minutes to an hour.

## Chickpeas (Garbanzo Beans)

High in protein, chickpeas are also a good source of calcium, iron, potassium, and B vitamins. They can be eaten hot, cold, or dried. They can be roasted like peanuts or boiled. You can make an assortment of pates with cooked chickpeas by adding a selection of nuts or vegetables.

### HUMMUS (CHICKPEA PUREE)
1. Mix lemon juice, garlic, mustard, chopped sweet onion, salt and pepper to taste with chickpeas.
2. Puree mixture in blender for a tart Middle-Eastern treat.

## Great Northern Beans

Great Northern beans and their small counterpart, navy beans, cook in less than an hour and require no pre-soaking. They are often used to make hearty soups.

## Lentils (Red, White, Yellow)

Lentils come in a variety of colors, but generally only the green, brown, and red varieties are available in the United States. All are nutritious sources of iron, cellulose, and B vitamins.

## Mung Beans

Mung beans are probably best known in their sprout form, eaten raw or lightly sautéd with other vegetables. Mung sprouts are rich in vitamins A and C and contain high amounts of calcium, phosphorous, and iron.

## Pinto Beans

Pinto beans are popular in American Southwest dishes, and lend themselves especially well to baking. Naturally sweet in flavor, they adapt to many types of seasonings, and once cooked tender, they can be used in casseroles.

## Soy Beans

Soybeans, unquestionably the most nutritious of all the beans, have been the major source of protein in Asian diets for centuries. In addition to high-quality protein, soybeans contain large amounts of B vitamins, minerals, and unsaturated fatty acids in the

form of lecithin that help the body emulsify cholesterol. Thanks to their bland flavor after cooking, soybeans can be made into an amazingly diverse array of
foods.

## Split Peas

Split peas, both green and yellow, make a simple soup
filled with protein and minerals. They do not require
soaking.

## *Nuts and Seeds*

Even if you're on a diet, nuts and seeds, though high
in calories, are marvelous foods. They're loaded with
essential fatty acids, high-quality protein, minerals (especially magnesium) and B vitamins, all of which are excellent for your heart, skin, brain, digestion, and regulate
your cholesterol.

Nuts contain good fats. A recent study performed
at Loma Linda University showed that among
Seventh-Day Adventists (who are vegetarians) those
who consumed five ounces of walnuts per week had a
substantial reduction in heart disease than those who
did not.

Nuts are versatile and can be eaten as a snack food
or added to other dishes to give crunch and flavor.
Instead of eating plain brown rice, try adding walnuts,
almonds, or sesame seeds and see how each transforms
the taste of a simple grain. For a sweet and crunchy
salad, add roasted nuts and oranges, seedless tanger-
ines, or pears to any grain.

> ### DRY ROASTED NUTS AND SEEDS
> 1. Place nuts or seeds of your choice on a baking sheet.
> 2. Sprinkle with soy sauce or sesame seed salt.
> 3. Bake at 450 degrees till browned. (Remember to check regularly to prevent seeds from burning.)

## Cashews

Cashews can be added to many dishes, whether layered in a casserole or simply roasted lightly. Cashew butter, from both raw and roasted nuts, is growing in popularity and is well-suited as an alternative to peanut butter to which many children have allergies.

> ### CASHEW BUTTER (RAW OR TOASTED)
> Throw cashews into blender or juice extractor until smooth. This popular spread can also be prepared adding a swirl of your favorite preserves. Spread on toasted bread.

> ### Difficulty in digesting nuts?
> Many nuts, including almonds and Brazil nuts, can be difficult to digest. Soaking them overnight in water makes them easy on any body.

CASHEW BUTTER MILK SHAKE

*Wow! What a delicious, nutrition-packed way to start the day.*

Combine:
2 cups rice or soy milk
1/2 cup cashew butter
2 tablespoons carob powder
Dash of vanilla
Pinch of nutmeg
1 teaspoon cinnamon
1 teaspoon protein powder
Pinch of salt

## Filberts (Hazelnuts)

Filberts are tasty nuts that, once chopped, make a delicious garnish for both greens and creamy tofu pudding. For those who are dieting: filberts contain an excess amount of calories for the amount of protein they provide.

## Pecans

High in potassium, B vitamins, and protein, pecans are delicious when tamari-roasted in a pan. In the shell, they can be kept for one year.

## Pignolias (Pine Nuts)

Not a good source of protein but a great source of minerals. Grown in the American Southwest, pignolias have been a staple in the Native American diet. You can pan-roast pine nuts and mix them with green vegetables such as peas and beans for a delicious, healthful dish.

## Pistachios

Raw pistachio nuts—not the salted ones you eat compulsively out of the shell—are rich in good oils and proteins.

## Pumpkin and Squash seeds

Rich in minerals, essential fatty acids, and zinc.

## Radish Seeds and Sprouts

Great for the intestines, radish seeds—both black and red—fight parasites in the intestines, bacterial infections, and food poisoning.

## Sesame Seeds (Benne)

Popular around the world for their high nutritional value—rich in niacin, vitamin E, magnesium, and calcium—great flavor and texture. Use hulled sesame seeds, which are more easily digested.

## Sunflower Seeds

One of the highest protein foods you can eat in a vegetarian diet. The sunflower takes approximately five months to grow and therefore absorbs a great supply of health-giving sunlight. The seeds are rich in unsaturated fatty acids, and are approximately 30 percent protein. For tasty, healthful snack, toast sesame seeds, season with garlic powder, and a variety of flavors.

Sunflower sprouts are the best of all the sprouts; nothing exceeds their nutritional value.

## Walnuts

Black walnuts are a real delicacy. They contain 40 percent more protein than English walnuts, also known as California walnuts. They last much longer when kept in the shell.

## Sprouts

With their bright green leaves, sprouts are rich in chlorophyll, an excellent detoxifier. And sprouted seeds are higher in vitamin C, minerals, and other enzymes than the food itself. Sunflower seeds, for example, are healthful but sunflower seed sprouts are about fifty times better.

About thirty different foods can be sprouted, including alfalfa, mung bean, buckwheat, quinoa, radishes—particularly good anticancer agents—mustard, and daikon. Sprouts vary in their sprouting time with most taking approximately three to five days. But sunflower seeds can take about seven days to sprout. You can purchase sprouting seeds in your local health food store.

---

### STEPS TO SPROUTING SEEDS

1. Add 4 parts water to 1 part seeds.
2. Soak the dried seeds for eight hours.
3. Rinse the seeds with cool water and place them in a sprouter.
4. Cut off the long shoots, which lack nutrition; it's the little green sprout at the top of the shoot that has the goods.
5. Add to salads, soups, and grains.

---

> ### *Seed Tip*
> **Save your seed-soaking water. It's great for cooking and watering plants.**

### Chia Seed and Sprouts

Chia seeds by weight have more nutrition than any other seed or nut. Chia belongs to a class of seeds called mucilage which become sticky when placed in water. Historically, Native Americans carried chia seeds in pouches, placing them under their tongue and allowing saliva to mix with the chia to form a gel that is packed with energy. The chia gelatin is neutral in flavor and can be used in a variety of dishes to boost nutrition. I throw some into my protein drink in the morning.

> ### CHIA SEED SPROUTS
> 1. Sprinkle the seeds over a saucer filled with water and allow to stand overnight.
> 2. By morning, the seeds will have absorbed all the water and will stick to the saucer.
> 3. Gently rinse and drain, using a sieve. Rinse twice daily.
> 4. After two to three days a small shoot will emerge. Harvest the seeds when the shoot is 1 inch long.

### Red Clover Sprouts

Red clover sprouts, though not widely consumed, are extremely healthful, similar in taste to alfalfa. In sprout form, this forage plant is an excellent source of chlorophyll.

RED CLOVER SPROUTS

1. Spread a handful of primary red clover leaves—about one inch in length—on a nonmetallic tray and dampen with water.
2. Cover with clear plastic to hold in the moisture.
3. Place in sunny spot for one to two hours until sprouted.

*Remember:*

**The more green you take in the more you're detoxifying.**

### Cress Seed Sprouts

Cress are tiny members of the mustard family. They add zest and taste to salads and dressings. Follow directions for sprouting chia seeds.

### Fenugreek Sprouts

Fenugreek seeds were first used to brew tea by ancient Greeks. This strong tea makes an excellent mouthwash, as well as a tasty and nutritious addition to soy or nut milk. When sprouted, fenugreek can be added to soups, salads, and grain dishes. The sprout should be harvested once it is 1/4 inch long.

### Flaxseed Sprouts

Flax, also known as linseed, has been used for centuries, as far back as the Greek and Roman empires. It makes a great laxative and cleanses the intestines.

Flaxseed is also pressed to make oil that is highly purifying. Follow direction for sprouting chia.

## Mustard Seed Sprouts

Spicy! Mustard seeds make a great flavor enhancer for salads and soups. Harvest when shoots are about one inch long.

## Barley Sprouts

Barley must be de-hulled before sprouting. It's best to purchase de-hulled barley from a seed company or suppliers of sprouting seeds. Barley sprouts are rich and aromatic. Cut with scissors and add to falafel, sandwiches, and salads.

## *Seaweed*

Seaweeds are sorely absent from the American diet—and what a loss it is! Seaweeds rank high as a basic source of essential minerals. They contain calcium, magnesium, phosphorous, potassium, iron, iodine, and sodium. Seaweed has only recently entered our cuisine, and it's high time. You can easily introduce seaweed to your family's diet.

### Agar (Kantan or Celanese Moss)

A translucent, almost weightless form of seaweed, agar can be purchased in many forms, including powdered, stick, or flakes. Agar is a natural thickener derived from vegetables—a great substitute for Jello, which is an animal product. Use it in fruit salads, to harden molds, puddings, soups, and to thicken drinks such as smoothies. To use as a thickener, dissolve about 1 ?-inch stick or 2 tablespoons of agar in a quart of any liquid to get a pudding-like consistency. The more agar you use, the more jellied the texture. After simmering, allow it to sit about 10 to 15 minutes to thicken, or place in refrigerator.

## Dulse

The only commercial sea vegetable available from the Atlantic Ocean, it's ready to eat when you buy it. You can put it into everything because it's almost tasteless. I add approximately 1/4 teaspoon to miso soup, vegetarian chili, and to carrot, cabbage, lentil, or potato leek soup to enhance nutritional value.

## Hijiki

A stringy, hair-like black seawood, hijiki has several nutrients, plus 57 percent more calcium by weight than dry milk. Hijiki must be soaked and rinsed in cold water two or three times before draining. Hijiki is best served when sautéd together with other vegetables—especially onions or leeks—or cooked with beans and grains.

## Kombu (Kelp)

Kombu is the Japanese term for several species of brown algae. Since kombu is especially rich in iodine, B-2, and calcium, it can help regulate an under-active thyroid gland, but consult your doctor before using it for this purpose.

## Nori (Dried Purple Laver)

The most popular of all Japanese seaweeds, nori comes in paper-thin dark purple sheets. Remarkably rich in protein, nori is also high in vitamins A, B-2, B-12, D, and niacin. You can roll tofu, brown rice and other grains, and cooked fish into the nori to make nori rolls.

## Wakame

A long seaweed with symmetrical and fluted fronds growing from both sides of an edible mid-rib, wakame looks a bit like green lasagna noodles. Rich in protein and niacin, wakame, in its dried state, contains almost 50 percent more calcium than dry milk. After soaking and cooking, wakame is excellent in miso soups. For a good elixir, mix tofu, shiitake mushrooms, garlic, liquid, and wakame into miso paste. Cook for five minutes. Let it steep and reduce. A terrific beverage to

> ### Seaweed Tip
>
> *All dried seaweeds increase greatly in size when you add water. For example, 1/4 cup of hijiki yields 1 cup when soaked. Save the soaking water for soup stock or for watering your garden vegetables, flowers, and shrubs. Plants love seaweed-soaked water.*

super-potentize your immune system—if you feel a cold or flu coming on, drink this; it's your best defense.

## Fermented Foods

Delicious miso and tamari are fermented seasonings derived from soybeans and other grains. They have a multitude of benefits that include helping to break down lactic acid, aiding digestion, creating good bacteria, and being rich in minerals. The fermenting process in the healthy human intestine isn't that different from what occurs in the production of soy foods. For example, maltose and glucose are broken down in your digestive tract to form lactic acid, ethyl alcohol, and organic acids. When we digest fermented foods, our bodies utilize microorganism cultures to synthesize these foods and help assimilate the nutrients we need. Miso, a soybean paste, is the most common fermented food in the world. Every Japanese or Chinese household stocks it.

Miso can be made from soybeans plus barley or rice; each has a different flavor. You can use miso in soups, dressings, or spreads for bread. It's wheat-free, and 18 percent complete protein. Tamari, a naturally fermented soy sauce, is high in sodium. Though I am opposed to salt-free diets, take care not to use too much tamari. Over-consumption of salt can lead to hypertension or kidney problems. When you use salt intelligently, it helps the body retain heat by slightly contracting the blood vessels, which is why we tend to consume more salt in cold months. It also helps maintain intestinal muscle tone by balancing the osmotic pressure—the pressure between the inside and outside of a cell—and electrical charges. Use some of the alternative seasonings listed below to cut down on salt (and sugar) and to get more flavor.

## Salt Alternatives
- Toasted sesame seeds combined with a small amount of sea salt
- Lemon juice with balsamic vinegar
- Umeboshi plums (small Japanese plums rich in citric acid which help to break down lactic acid and counteract sugar)

## Sugar Alternatives

*Honey.* Use only raw, unfiltered, and unheated honey for its natural enzymes. Honey comes in many flavors depending upon the source of the bee's nectar. Historically, honey has been the most commonly used medicine since it has natural antibiotic, antibacterial qualities. Honey taken with herbal tea coats a sore throat, thereby killing the bacteria.

*Granulated Date Sugar.* You can buy pre-ground date sugar or grind your own dried dates into a powder.

*Dry-Roasted Carob Powder.* A delicious sweetener, brown carob powder makes a terrific powdered chocolate substitute.

*Grain Sweeteners.* Rice syrup (ame in Japanese) and barley malt (note: avoid if allergic to barley)

*Blackstrap Molasses.* Produced in one of the intermediate stages of sugar refining, molasses contains about 35 percent sucrose. It is rich in iron, calcium and B vitamins.

*Barbados.* A milder, dark brown molasses with a higher sucrose content than blackstrap.

*Sorghum.* A molasses made from the sorghum plant, it has a distinctive taste; better for baking than consuming raw.

> ## Sugar substitutes to avoid:
>
> **Raw, turbinado, and brown sugars are still as high as 96 percent sucrose (processed sugar is 99 percent).**

## Oils

### Olive Oil

Olive oil is by far the best all-around oil. Use it every day in salads and for cooking. Because olive oil imparts such great taste, use it at the end of cooking. If used at the beginning it can easily be scorched. Unrefined safflower oil is a good cooking oil because it can withstand higher temperatures without losing its chemical and nutritional makeup.

### Safflower, Sunflower, Sesame, and Soybean Oils

The best cooking oils are mild and almost odorless. At the end of cooking, when you want to impart flavor, add a toasted sesame or safflower oil. Again, avoid use at the beginning because these sensitive oils can be easily scorched.

## *Teas*

*Bancha.* Make sure your diet contains Bancha tea which is high in calcium.

*Dark Green Tea (Chinese Green Tea).* High in cancer-preventing properties.

*Herbal Teas.* Drink herbal teas everyday, including mint (good for digestion), kava, valerian root (if you're feeling a little stressed), or any herb you enjoy.

## *Baking Powders*

These are used as leavening agents in "quick bread"—a bread that can be baked in less than half an hour. Quick breads lend themselves to concentrated nutrients such as seeds and nuts. You can use a variety of flours, including triticale, soy, brown rice, and millet. Never use sodium bicarbonate to make quick breads since it is high in sodium. Instead use low-sodium, aluminum-free (remember, aluminum is toxic) potassium bicarbonate.

## *Natural Thickeners*

To thicken sauces and soups, use a finely ground starch flour such as rice flour with any of a variety of natural thickeners such as arrowroot powder or kudzu root.

## Vinegar

Never use white distilled or wine varieties of vinegar, which are acidic. Refined distilled vinegar has few nutrients and virtually none of the identifiable subtle flavors of the naturally aged vinegars. Instead, use apple cider vinegar made from whole, unsprayed, and naturally aged apples. Apple cider vinegar contains malic acid, which when used wisely is a constructive acid that aids the digestive system.

# Step #5:

## Exercise for Rejuvenation

The rewards of exercise are immediate and enduring. Regular exercise is essential for getting yourself into peak condition. It increases your metabolism to help you lose or maintain your weight, and can help prevent disease by releasing toxins such as carbon dioxide. Exercise will balance your body's enzymes, nutrients, and minerals, giving you more energy, more vitality, and clearer, more vibrant skin. In this section you'll find a wide range of exercises, easily applied. They're all low-impact, so there's minimal chance of injury and maximum benefit.

## *Before You Begin*

Every exercise regimen should begin with a doctor's check-up to make sure you have no cardiovascular disease or hidden high blood pressure that could be a risk factor in an exercise program.

Ideally, you'll also want to take an "impedance" test that measures body fat, lean muscle, and water. If you're a woman, your fat level should be somewhere in the teens, and if you're a man, your fat level should range between nine and thirteen. The lower the fat and the higher the muscle-to-fat ratio, the healthier you're going to be. Once you know your fat level versus the ideal level, you'll know what to aim for.

## *Getting Optimal Benefit from Your Workout*

*Time.* The average workout should last about forty-five minutes to an hour each day. That includes ten minutes of stretching to warm up and ten minutes of slow movement to cool down. Never stop exercising suddenly; allow your heart and other systems to slow down gradually.

*Pulse.* Before starting, always take your wrist pulse for sixty seconds. Exercise at 75 percent of your optimal level, which can be determined by subtracting your age from 220 and multiplying that by 75. That will give you the ideal number of heartbeats per minute. It may take you a while to reach that level. That's okay, just work toward that goal.

*Getting hydrated.* Make sure you are properly hydrated by drinking lots of pure water and juices. Fresh-squeezed juices contain electrolytes, which are integral to the transmission of nerve impulses and good muscular function. Juices should be taken before and after a workout. Unfortunately, many people don't drink enough before exercising and can dehydrate. When you're dehydrated, your electrolytes become unbalanced and the electrical charges in your brain don't fire properly, which can cause forgetfulness and fatigue. Drink up!

*Power food.* Ingest complex carbohydrates, such as a brown rice protein drink. Before exercising, to get the energy you'll need. After a workout, preferably within a half hour of exercise, have some protein. Protein supplies amino acids which penetrate the cells and expand the protoplasm, giving you energy to get through the exercise. Taking in protein after exercise helps the body expand muscle mass.

*After exercising.* After your workout, take a warm bath in Epsom salts or get a massage to relax your muscles. Do not go into a hot bath, hot tub, or steam room, which could raise your already high blood temperature even higher. Exercise also raises your pulse rate and your blood pressure; a hot bath will take those numbers even higher. Instead, take a tepid—not hot—shower to help you cool down.

*Mood enhancement.* There are few more sure-fire mood elevators than aerobic exercise—it's terrific for everything that ails you. Aerobic exercise will help get you into a positive frame of mind by stimulating endorphins, the brain hormones of mood. For the six hours follows your workout, your mind and body will feel clear and elevated. To help your endorphins along, try not to introduce negative thoughts and problems while you work out. Focus on what you're doing at the moment, and if you're fortunate enough to be in natural surroundings, experience nature—the birds singing, the breezes, the warmth of the sun, the trees and flowers. Holding on to positive images will help your mind as well as your body, giving you a more complete sense of well-being.

*Exercise consistently.* If you keep up a regular exercise regimen you'll notice positive changes in the way you look and feel. I've started lots of people on health programs—I never put anyone on a diet—with exercise being a key component, and they all lose weight easily. You lose weight because exercise speeds up your metabolism. You feel better and gain more confidence. Many people I've worked with have gone from being out of shape to becoming champion athletes, with some ranking among the best athletes in the United States today. Your goal may not be to become a top athlete, but you can certainly improve your physique and health to a great degree. With almost daily exercise—I recommend exercising six days a week and taking a day off to rest—you can bring down your blood pressure and cholesterol into the normal, healthy range, and have your body burning calories more efficiently all day long, including when you're asleep.

*Pacing.* Begin by exercising moderately. Increasing gradually over a period of time will increase your endurance, then your stamina, and finally your pace. Visualize yourself a year from now: Not only will you like what you see when you look in the mirror, but you'll feel different, more alive. You'll have more energy and a brighter outlook.

### Aerobic Exercises

Aerobic exercise moves major muscle groups in a rhythmic manner that sends more oxygen through the body for greater energy. As more blood is pumped to the heart and cells, toxins such as carbon dioxide are readily released from the system, making aerobic exercise a natural detoxifier. Choose from a variety of aerobic exercises— power walking, running, bicycling, swimming, or cross-country skiing, for example— but make one of these activities, or better yet, a combination, a part of your regular routine. Start slowly and build your endurance and skill.

### Power Walking

Power walking makes a great workout: it's easy to learn and virtually anyone can do it. Plus, power walking is low-impact. You won't injure yourself as you could easily do while jogging. In addition, when you power walk you work many different muscle groups to produce a total musculoskeletal workout. Power walking also enhances cardiovascular health, as well as burns fat. You can vary your pace to one that suits you—slow or quick—and still benefit, making it a perfect exercise for everyone, young and old.

Let's look at the proper form and get started.

In power walking, there are only a few rules to follow regarding form and movement. When you are power walking properly, your shoulders are relaxed. Your ears are lined up with the shoulders, not craned forward; otherwise, you'll strain your lower back. Lean your whole body forward at a 5-degree angle. It may help you to visualize someone pulling a string that is attached to your head and shoulders up and forward at a 5-degree angle. The arms drive you. As you speed up the power and pace of your arms, you increase your aerobic exercise. (Many people walk with their arms across their chest, but that's wrong.) Hips and shoulders are relaxed, and you're leaning forward. Let the hips flow, almost like a Marilyn Monroe walk, or a samba. Let it flow and glide. Raising your hip slightly and extending your leg out gives you a longer stride. Also, when you raise your hip and extend your leg you're using your thigh and gluteus muscles, making them firm. If you don't use the hips, you're merely raising your legs up and down, without using as many muscles.

When you step, your foot should land on the heel and push off the toe. (Power walking is frequently called heel-and-toe.) The last thing you feel is your big toe pushing off. Normally, you land on the middle of the foot. In power walking, you want to be far more efficient. Eventually, power walking will develop your calves and give you added strength. Keep the feet close to the ground, making nice, close, smooth movements.

For optimal benefit, breathe deeply through the mouth, not the nose. When you breath through the mouth, more oxygenated blood nourishes all the capillaries and cells of the body, and more waste is released. Deep breathing prevents lactic acid buildup in tight muscles. Deep breathing is about half the benefit you'll get from exercise.

Why is power walking so beneficial? First, you're burning more calories per muscle group than you are when running. In addition to building strong legs and calves, you're also developing better chest, shoulder, and back muscles with your arm movements. In running, you're developing only your legs; but with power walk-ing, you're using all the muscles, and burning fat, building

muscle, and getting cardiovascular conditioning.
Benefits will occur gradually. Don't rush it. Work at one single distance for about a month. The next month, increase your distance. A month after that, walk farther still. By the fourth month, increase your speed. Don't rush it. With power walking, speed doesn't count. It's about endurance and aerobic cardiovascular conditioning. You want to condition the muscles gradually.

## Osteoporosis and Power Walking

*Power walking is one of the best preventives for osteoporosis. When your body is relaxed and breathing rhythmically, much-needed calcium is being forced into the long bones, preventing them from breaking down. In addition, walking stimulates the immune system, detoxifies the body, helps to eliminate edema, and, over time, assists in lowering blood pressure and cholesterol. Power walking also helps stimulate your mood. Have you heard of a runner's high? Well, you can get a walker's high, too.*

## Jogging

Jogging or running won't injure your body, as long as you use correct form and technique. Let's look at some of the errors people commonly make and ways to avoid them:

*Legs low.* When jogging, people generally tend to raise their legs too high. In effect, they bounce. That's fine for sprinters running a 50- or 100-yard dash. But if you're going out for a four-, five-, or six-mile run, raising your legs and pounding them down can cause injury. This is especially true if you are running downhill. Remember, the hill is down, but your leg is going out. That results in great impact. When jogging, you place a good deal of pressure per square inch on your joints, especially your knees and ankles.

*Good form.* Power walking and running are similar in form. The arm is used as a balance, with the wrist bone at the hip-bone level. Don't move your arm much—only far enough so that if you were to take a handkerchief out of your front pocket you could easily put it in your back pocket. When running, your ears are lined up with your shoulders, and your body is at the same five-degree angle as in power walking. Breathe deeply with your mouth open on exhaling.

The closer the feet are to the ground the less impact on the joints. Don't take long strides. Keep your strides comfortable. When you go up or down a hill, shorten your strides and tilt your elbow up. When you elevate your elbows in this way your body automatically leans into the field of gravity. Lean into the hill whether going up or down.

*Loose legs.* To keep pressure off the leg, don't run stiff-legged. Many people do, and it jars all the glands, the organs, and bones. You want just a slight bend in the knee, about a quarter of an inch, just enough so that there is buoyance and shock absorbency. If you're landing near the heel and pushing off gradually, then the shock should go out, outside of the calf, through the quads, and out the gluteus (your buttock muscle). When you land, you should be able to strike the ground near the back and slightly to the right of the heel. If you look at the heel of your running shoe, and it is worn down on one side, it is likely that you are pronating, or rotating out. This should—and can—be avoided as it can cause injury.

If you tend to pronate, see a sports podiatrist to determine if you should be fitted for an orthotic—a little cup that's inserted into the shoe to hold the foot in proper position. Then, when you do land, you won't go off to one side or the other. You can also buy shoes that are air-cushioned. The cushion absorbs the shock. Air-cushioned shoes have a wedge that positions the heel at an angle instead of straight. By having your heel and shoe at an angle, they are automatically balanced and you are less likely to end up with pronation. Get new running shoes after you put 700-800 miles on them to avoid losing proper pressure absorbency. Shoes are not that expensive and they're really the only piece of equipment in running. Learn good running habits, and jogging can be a fun way to stay fit.

### Aerobic Exercise Tip

*Be sure to keep hydrated, take your pulse before and after, and gradually increase your endurance before you focus on speed.*

## Bicycling

Alternating between running and bike riding will provide a total workout for the legs. Running builds the rear leg muscles and bicycling strengthens the front of the legs. Varying your routine with two exercises lessens the chance of injury to the joints and muscles.

For best aerobic results, ride at a steady pace bringing your heart rate into the middle of your target range. Moving too slowly won't give you the desired cardiovascular benefits quickly enough.

When bicycling outdoors, take safety precautions. Most important, protect your head with a safety helmet. Even the most experienced rider can tumble after hitting a hairline crack on the road or a slick of black ice. In addition, you'll need quality biking shoes, or at the very least good running or walking shoes, and foot clips to prevent your feet from slipping off the pedals. Your bicycle should be the appropriate height for your body (you can consult with your bike dealer to determine the correct size) and built on a strong, solid frame. Many women prefer bikes designed for men since the extra bar adds stability to the frame. Adjust the seat to the correct height. To determine correct height, make sure that

### Biking Safety Precautions

*At dusk and in the dark, wear light-colored and reflective clothing, and put a reflector on your bike. When riding on the road, follow the direction of traffic.*

when your foot is on the pedal, your knee is only slightly bent when you reach the pedal's lowest point.

On stationary bikes, the best form is the sitting-up position, not bent over as on a racing bike. Be sure to pedal hard enough to get an aerobic benefit. Always keep spinning at a regular pace in a continuous motion. This will build up your endurance and make you a stronger biker.

## Swimming

Swimming provides a high-energy cardiovascular workout while strengthening the arms, shoulders, and rear leg muscles. Water keeps resistance low, making this an especially good sport for people suffering from injuries or structural problems that prevent them from engaging in most land sports.

If you don't swim, try walking in a pool several times with water at waist height. Build up to your target heart rate and sustain that level for at least 20 minutes. You can also run in deep water wearing a life vest. This is especially good for building up the legs after a leg injury, or as an addition to a running program.

## Cross-Country Skiing

Try this sport for a total muscle workout; cross-country skiing utilizes every major muscle group in the body. Don't let the lack of snow stop you. An indoor cross-country ski machine is an excellent substitute. Those who know claim you'll get even greater benefit from this activity than you will from running.

## Jumping Rope

If your goal is to lose weight, consider jumping rope. Jumping burns more calories in a shorter time than any other workout. It's quite strenuous, however, so be sure to start slowly and build up gradually, otherwise, you could injure yourself.

Start by jumping for just a few minutes, no more than three or four, less if you're older. Start by walking or running in place, speeding up until your feet leave the ground quickly. Be light-footed. Now jump on both feet at the same time for ten to thirty seconds with or without a rope.

## Anaerobic Exercise

Anaerobic literally means "without oxygen." Anaerobic exercises include workouts that require quick bursts of energy, such as lifting weights, or sprinting. The body's existing oxygen, along with the energy produced by muscle cells that require no oxygen, enables us to perform short, intense tasks. However, we can do this for only short periods of time before we run out of steam. For a total workout, you'll need to complement your aerobic program with anaerobic training.

### Weight Training

One way to condition every part of your body is to train with weights. Properly performed, weight training will not give you a muscle-bound physique, and will make you stronger and better conditioned. There's equipment, both free weights (also known as dumbbells) and gym machines, for toning every part of your body.

For optimum conditioning, all the muscles in your

body should be exercised. Toning muscles—and general physical fitness— can stem the tide of aging and help ward off the illnesses associated with the aging process. From your nose to your toes, every muscle group has to be exercised.

Whether you exercise in a gym or at home, when you work with weights, it's good to get the help of a physical trainer to better understand what you are doing and how to do it properly. To create a home gym, buy some inexpensive free weights, and perhaps a slant board and a sit-up machine. A home gym is wonderful in that it frees you to exercise any time, day or night. To stay motivated, you might pair up with a friend or family member and set up workout times. The main motivation, however, will come from you.

Weight lifting is a gradual program. Avoid working strenuously until you're physically capable, which takes time. Lifting weights exercises specific muscle groups, burning the fat in that group. Your muscles are already saturated with fat, so when there's no more room, the fat starts spilling over. At this point, though you may do all the sit-ups in the world, you're still going to have fat on your stomach. Sit-ups won't get rid of that. That fat on top of the muscle belongs to the whole body. To rid yourself of this overfat, do aerobic exercises which burn up excess fat in the body, speeding up the metabolism.

For best results, work at a level you can handle and then move up, slowly, from there. A good regimen consists of doing three different sets of each exercise. Start at ten repetitions (reps)—which constitutes a set; do three sets, or a total of thirty reps, per each exercise. Then wait sixty seconds until your lactic acid flushes out and you feel relaxed before moving on to your next exercise. In time you can increase the weight and the number of reps in your sets. A year from now you might be doing four or five sets at fifteen to twenty reps.

Women, unlike men, will not become muscle-bound from lifting weights, especially if they do not lift a lot of weight. Women have less lean muscle tissue than men and more fat cells. Women who lift weights become strong and tight and burn up cellulite. You'll have nice abs (abdominal muscles), and nice pecs (pectoral muscles). Your chest muscles will begin to tighten up, toning your breasts. Your posture will improve and you'll avoid that humped look that can come with aging.

Working with resistance and weights increases lymphatic flow which is so beneficial to your breasts. Build-up of lymphatic fluid is one of the contributing factors to breast cancer and autotoxemia. Make sure you work on the following muscle groups for a comprehensive anaer-obic workout:

- Stomach
- Chest
- Arms
- Leg
- Back
- Shoulder

There are many exercises you can do for aerobic enhancement and strength building. When you get on a regular regimen, you will feel better than you've ever felt before. It's worth it.

## Breathing

**When doing any resistance exercises, always remember to breathe properly. Exhale through your mouth upon rising or lifting, and inhale through your nose when coming down. Breathing right brings rich oxygen to the muscles and makes exercising more efficient and easier.**

### Yoga

As an adjunct to aerobic and anaerobic exercises, yoga offers a non-impact system of both mental and physical exercises.

Yoga brings body, mind, and spirit together into a state of harmony. Breath and breathing practices are the source of yoga's benefits, helping circulation and collecting toxins so that they can be exhaled. Yoga has many proven benefits, including decreasing insulin dependence in diabetics, and the frequency of asthma attacks. Yoga is a powerful antidote to depression, anxiety, and panic as it teaches you how to reduce stress by releasing the tension in your mind and body.

It's best to begin a yoga program by taking classes from a certified yoga instructor so that you're assured of doing the exercises properly.

# Step #6:

## De-Stressing Your Life

Stress is the most pervasive emotional problem of our age. And small wonder. We are burdened with an overwhelming drive to achieve more: to do more than we can—in the shortest period of time—and to have more than we need or even want. We believe that the more we have, the more we accomplish; the more we achieve, the more people will respect us. Many people work overtime to get there. As a result, we have lost many of the fulfillments and connections to ourselves that a simpler life had provided for us in the past. I'm not suggesting we turn back the clock, but rather to look at it, and create our own schedule.

There are several excellent strategies for coping with stress, including yoga and meditation. But the best and most effective way toward well-being is through knowing what we as individuals truly value and truly need. Much in the same way that eating a diet rich in fat and sugar ends up starving your body of the vital nutrients necessary for good health, when you're not getting what you need out of life—when you struggle in a career that doesn't really please you or a relationship that isn't right for you—your soul becomes starved and you feel a constant, underlying discomfort. This pervasive feeling makes you more susceptible to stress, and dealing with problems as small as not being able to find a parking space or as big as deciding to change jobs can become equally paralyzing.

I want to show you a completely different way of approaching your life so that you will not become stressed to begin with. I want to show you that just "being" is enough; that you don't have to do anything special to enjoy the uniqueness of your existence. Though this philosophy does not fare well in our society—"I'm working two shifts to buy that big house. Why aren't you?" or, "Why are you wasting your time meditating in the afternoon?"—it will do wonders for you. Through a reevaluation of your accepted beliefs, goals, and behavior (which are the result of conditioning rather than choice) by knowing your own heart and mind better, you will achieve inner balance.

Ask yourself the questions listed below and you will begin to open your mind to who you really are, instead of who you believe you're supposed to be. By gaining your sense of identity from internal processes you will truly nourish yourself and find well-being.

## *Who determines what you expect of yourself?*

How much of what you do depends upon what you believe is expected of you? Perhaps you haven't pursued careers, talents, or relationships with people because of unconscious notions of what you "should" do, rather than what feels right for you. We are conditioned to believe that there is a "right way of living," regardless of what we value as individuals. Sometimes we don't even know what matters to us because those answers have been supplanted by all the "shoulds" and "musts" we are given. Usually those "shoulds" are about external things, like what we should wear, who should be our friends, or how much money should we have.

The only way to change your expectations so that they reflect your true values is to ask yourself: Do I really believe I need to be a corporate vice president to be happy? Why do I think that I do? What work do I really want to do? It's better to build on what you love. My own standard of living comes from the joy and passion I receive from my work. Nothing I do takes away from who I am, and I don't have to own anything to feel complete. That's the difference between focusing on an internal process of being and concentrating on external achievements. One connects you to yourself, the other takes you away. Disease often takes hold when we're not honoring who we really are.

## *What defines your sense of self?*

Career? Money? Appearance? Many people believe they are what they do or what they have; that they are their public identity, the label they wear. If they have the right job, the right car, the right home and children, then they know who they are. But what happens when one of those elements is not right? The divorce rate, after all, is more than 50 percent. If you define yourself by these externals, you won't be able to feel good about yourself if one of these things goes wrong.

## Do you understand the importance of now?

Look at now, right now. All your opportunities for creating joy are in *this moment*, not in the future. Too often, people become preoccupied with the future and lose sight of the now. When we're children, our parents always ask us what we want to be when we grow up. Just when we're enjoying the moment—riding a horse, ice-skating—or reading a book, adults feel compelled to make predictions about our future. What does this do? It creates the mindset that what we are living now isn't enough, that it's got to become some "thing" in order to be real: a label, a title, a career, something other than pure experience. If you're always looking toward the future, you can never have what you have.

All we have are moments. When we can be fully engaged and aware in the moment, it will last in our memory for a lifetime and its pleasure becomes embedded in our very cells. Once you start seeing how much joy you can create by being present, you can stop looking for that happiness in some elusive future.

## Can you embrace change?

When you're not looking toward the future, are you too fixed on the past? On how great you looked when you were younger? On your first kiss? On the play you starred in when you were in fifth grade? On your last job? If your gaze is always set on fixed reference points in the past, your expectation is that you can have the same experience again. That isn't possible, and believing it is holds you back from new experiences. As one Greek philosopher said, "You never put your foot in the same river twice." No two kisses are the same. No two meals are the same, even if you follow the same recipe. Change is the only constant in life.

Assuming that our beliefs are permanent will limit our growth. Embrace change. Every breath you breathe is a new one. Surrender your need to repeat what you know and you will be able to flow with life, rather than resist it. If you want to grow, you must surrender to change.

### Do you always compare yourself to others?

When a friend buys a new house or apartment, a new car, or when their children attend private schools or dress more expensively than yours, do you begin to feel anxious that you're missing out on something? Or doing something wrong? Comparing yourself to others will always leave you feeling deprived. After all, you can't become full by watching someone else eat. If you always measure yourself by what others do, you lose contact with yourself. And when you lose that vital connection you cannot experience the pleasure of your own being. No matter how much you have or don't have, you will always feel deprived. Likewise, satisfaction does not come with wanting—or having— what others have. Ask yourself what you really value, what you really need to live your own life. It may be quite different than what other people would say.

Whether your children go to public or private school is a matter of choice, of what you value in their education. There is no guarantee that a private education will be a better one. Your participation in your child's education, your pleasure in learning, and your support of your child's pleasure in learning are as, if not more, significant than the school they go to. Perhaps you would like a bigger apartment? But what would you have to give up to get one?

Ask yourself what, deep down, really fulfills you. Do you like to write or love to read? Perhaps you delight in taking long walks in the park or cooking beautiful meals or listening to a great piece of music. Sharing experiences with good, close friends is a joy that money can't buy.

No one is happier or feels less deprived than the person who can take pleasure in what really feeds their individual soul. You cannot buy that gift. Nurture your own pleasures, instead of comparing yourself to others. Ask yourself, "What do I need to honor who I am?" and you will have everything.

### Where does fear come from?

Fear is a natural response to a sense of danger to the self. Young babies, at a certain developmental stage, will cry when they do not see their mother; their natural helplessness and their identification of self and security through the mother, makes them anxious when Mother—their protector—is out of sight.

As adults, however, many of our fears are not natural, but conditioned responses from childhood. We become afraid because at some time in our life we were judged harshly for our choices. As children, if we were criticized for the way we expressed ourselves, wore our hair or clothes, how colorful our clothes were, or how we kept our rooms, we became afraid of not being good enough. We feared we would be rejected or abandoned. When we're grown, that fear remains with us and makes us afraid to do many things, without knowing exactly what we're afraid of. We hesitate to speak our minds for fear we may say something wrong and incur someone's anger. We don't ask for a raise or a vacation for fear of disapproval and the possibility of losing our jobs.

By realizing that the true roots of our fears are in the past—and that we survived those fearful times and became adults—we can accept that we are no longer helpless and dependent on others for our survival and can therefore be who we are. We can speak our minds and ask for what we feel entitled to. Knowing that there is no cause to fear our current situation, we can handle whatever comes, because we don't need the approval of others to live.

## Do you solve problems or just fear them?

If you discover that you have a medical condition or that a project you're working on is falling through, do you panic? Like the Pavlovian dog, many people automatically react to problems by becoming anxious or overexcited. The degree of anxiety you experience in response to problems reflects a conditioned fear that you are not capable of solving problems and cannot trust yourself. In essence, what you fear is being out of control of your life. Getting nervous, you believe, will give you back control: "Uh-oh, trouble, I've lost control.

Get nervous. That will mean I'm doing something." The next time you panic, ask yourself, "How will getting nervous or stressed help me solve the problem?" Better yet, think of how it might get in the way. Remaining calm frees your mind to think of options and be available to those who may need you in a crisis.

In the end all problems get resolved, sometimes because of what we do, sometimes despite what we do. We have only limited control. What's most important is that you ask yourself why you feel the need to become over-stressed when faced with a problem. When you can answer this you will become a much better—and calmer—problem solver.

## Do you feel you deserve what you really want?

This is the one question you must answer even before you can ask yourself what you want. It's difficult to pursue your goals if deep down you don't feel entitled even to have them. You may fail to do the work you want to do, to find the partner you'd like to have, to be the weight you'd like to be, and be unaware that the reason these things elude you is because you don't feel deserving. In the end, you're only going to allow yourself to have what you feel you deserve. But who decided what you deserve? Did you? And how did you come to that determination?

Sid Howard came to my first class on the boardwalk in Brooklyn twenty-five years ago and said, "Gary, I want to be as healthy as a human being can be." I said, "All right, Sid, that's a big challenge because to do that you have to know that you can do it, and that there is no inherent reason, barring extraordinary circumstances, why you cannot.

You must silence any voices in your head that question you and say, "Why should you feel so good? What makes you think you're worthy of it?"

At the age of sixty, Sid now has the body of a 35-year-old. And it's all because he believes in, and is still proving each day, his right to be who he wants to be. He believes he deserves to be that healthy. Your ability to set goals and achieve them is not contingent on anything other than desire. Rich or poor, fat or thin, tall or short, as a member of the human race you deserve to fulfill your goals. You don't have to be special in any way to be deserving. Every human being is entitled to happiness.

## Do you need someone to love you to feel self-worth?

Connection to yourself and to others is perhaps the most life-affirming experience in our lives. However, many of us seek the love of others not for affirmation of life but because of social expectations: You're supposed to be part of a couple; if not, you're a loser and are doomed to be lonely. So many single people are deprived of the great pleasure to be taken in solitary pursuits because of these attitudes. Solitude is an important component of life, allowing us to replenish ourselves after spending our days giving and doing things for others. We cannot be of much use to the world if we've used up our own vital energy.

Many people also seek love not just to be socially acceptable but because they feel empty or unfulfilled and believe that it takes someone else, a lover, to fill their needs. But love is not love if you love someone because you need them. Love is love when you need someone because you love them.

You are the only one who can fill your own needs. No

one else knows better than you what you need. You can be in a relationship and still feel insecure. You'll never believe you are whole until you create that wholeness.

## Do you see your glass as half-full or half-empty?

Most people tend to focus on what they lack, either in themselves or in their lives. The only way to fight that tendency is to learn that your glass is always half-full. You do so by replacing others' perceptions of what constitutes fullness with your own. Be positive instead of negative. Instead of saying, "I haven't been to the gym in three months and I'm too lazy to go back," why not remind yourself of all those years you were going regularly? Use your accomplishments to bolster you through a rough patch, rather than focusing only on the rough patch and seeing it as your whole life. Even if you're not in the mood, pick yourself up and go for a workout. Once you're in the gym, suddenly all those years of feeling the endorphin high and the satisfaction of feeling in shape will come right back to you. Good feelings will always crowd out the bad. So, simply replace bad feelings with good ones and your cup will "runneth over."

## Are you easily provoked?

Your stress level is not contingent on external events. Certainly your patience or calm will be tested or influenced when your boss has words with you or when your car breaks down, but your degree of anxiety in response to those events is determined by your belief system.

"But Gary," you'll say, "that's not true. When someone

jumps in front of me on line for a movie, or someone gives me a bad look, they're provoking me, causing me to . . ." No, they're causing nothing. It's your reaction to what you can't control that creates the stress and frustration. Try accepting that you don't have full control over what happens—only your response—and see how easily your anxiety melts away. Change your reaction, and you change your world.

## Do you believe you can achieve balance in your life?

The only goal worth striving for is balance. What do I mean? Let's say you want to win big running the marathon. Even if you come in first, if you achieve that by collapsing on the finish line, have you really won? You may think so, but what if you become ill and can't get out of bed for the next week? Have you still won? You may have won the race, but you've lost your well-being. Which is worth more?

Once again that phenomenon of external reality comes back at us again. If you're focused only on external realities, you'll say you won and that's all that counts, even though you feel miserable the rest of the time and may even have done damage to your body. That can't be what we're trying to achieve in the race. And, I assume, that's not what attracted you to entering the race.

You want to feel less stressed, more balanced. If you come in the race as number 100 but you feel great along the way, you've won a great victory. You've won a balanced life. It's not the end that counts; it's the process. And life is the ultimate process.

## *Are you a self-actualizer?*

Self-actualizers are people who do things so that they can develop their experience of life. Do you set high goals for yourself? If you do, how do you go about achieving them? And if you're not an achiever, how are you ever going to grow? You've got to be an achiever. What I mean by achievement is really self-actualization. It's not what you achieve outside that matters; accomplishment is measured by how much you grow inside. But to achieve inside, you've got to surrender your expectations of material rewards. There's nothing wrong with achieving something—winning a race, getting a promotion—if it mirrors your inner self. As long as it's harmony and balance you're striving for, then your achievements will not be built on superficial expectations. That's healthy. That's vital.

## *Do you value the small, pleasurable events in your daily life?*

Change your daily routine. Make every day a ritual of happiness. Think in terms of simple acts, things you can easily do. Play with your pet. Spend some time planting flowers, or grow sprouts, or listen to music; indulge in those hobbies. Go to a quiet place and read or, if it's warm, just feel the sun, the warmth. Take in the aromas of your surroundings. Make a new dish from a new cookbook. All of these are easy things to do, and don't take the whole day. Take time for simple pleasures throughout the day: Write your friends short letters or e-mails; buy flowers. When you create new, satisfying rituals, you reconnect with your inner self. It's when we lose our connection with our own feelings that we become anxious, lost, and depressed. Connect. Make the day happen for you.

## Do you have a distorted view of yourself?

Do you see yourself for who you are? Or do you see yourself for who you were told you are? When you were little, did you have any doubt that you were a complete, loving, whole human being? If yes, how does this manifest itself now? If you don't see yourself accurately, what do you see about yourself? Do you not see your potential? Do you not see your completeness? Do you see your joy? Do you see your creativity? You won't find what you don't see and what you haven't been encouraged to look at. That's why you need new tools, a new way of thinking about what matters to you and why. Questioning your automatic thoughts about your life, understanding what you truly value, rather than what you have been conditioned to value, are vital tools to help you create a new mindset and live closer to your heart and mind. With that new mindset, we begin to see in our ourselves what we need to feel well, and, amazingly, we find it.

## Step #7:

### Taking Charge of Your Perfect Health

Imagine that you are about to walk across America. Let's say that only by walking to the other side of the continent will you find health and well-being. If you stay where you are you will continue to be burdened with chronic problems, such as fatigue, pain, and depression. So all you have to do to remedy those problems is to put one foot in front of another, take one step at a time, and stay focused on your goal.

You have been equipped with information about the conditions of the crossing, you have been told what you will find along the way, and you have been given the tools you'll need to give you stamina. Take that first step. Now you can take the journey.

Do you believe you can do it? There's no doubt it's difficult to have the faith and confidence that you'll make it; after all, you've never done this before. There will certainly be challenges. On the other hand, you only have to take one step at a time. And if you succeed, your life will change immeasurably. Not only will you feel great energy and endurance, you'll learn about yourself and a better way to live your life.

You can do it. Just make the choice to make a move and, most importantly, be patient with yourself. Making the decision to take this journey means you're taking charge of your life. And taking charge is one of the most important steps you'll ever take toward health and well-being. Think of all the crises you've been through because you haven't taken care of yourself: persistent illnesses, stress, and unhappiness. Are you finally at the breaking point? Are you ready to say, "Enough! I'm willing to change to feel better"? Everything depends upon making this choice.

### Conquer Your Fears

Many people have great difficulty taking responsibility for caring for themselves. We all wish someone else would do for us what our parents did when we were children. Yet even as children we had to learn to do things for ourselves. As an adult, at one time or another, you may feel too physically weak, too alone, or too emotionally helpless to help yourself. The fact remains, though, that no one can do for you what you must do for yourself; it would be like asking someone to brush our teeth for us, or eat our food. Your most vital needs can be filled only by you. When you fail to do so you deprive yourself and become sick.

This is exactly the pattern that *The 7 Steps to Perfect Health* will help you conquer. Once you start this program, beginning with the ideas in Step 1, you will immediately feel stronger because you have taken a step toward your own well-being.

## *Change: Your Life May Depend on it*

I've counseled many people who have been told by their physicians that they have a terminal illness and there are no more treatments available to help them. As a last resort they come to see me, and they're frightened. Yet when I offer them other options and show them how alternatives to traditional medicine have helped others in their situation, they have difficulty following through. They're frightened by what they don't know, and by anything that is different. This is normal. Don't they want to change? I truly believe they do, but I also believe they don't feel empowered to make their own choices and, in their feelings of disempowerment, they fall back on what everyone else is doing. They do this not only because it seems safe (and undemanding), but because they have fixed ideas that it is the right thing to do. Yet, by remaining fixed on the status quo, by not attempting to look beyond your preconceptions, you miss the opportunity to change, perhaps even, in some cases, to save your life.

We are conditioned to believe that traditional medicine knows everything about the workings of the human body; it's considered the gold standard. Yet many doctors of traditional medicine will admit that even they do not understand how a particular medication works, only that it does, illustrating the limits to our understanding of certain diseases. There are also many doctors who were once completely resistant to natural cures and treatments who are now slowly being convinced—by powerful evidence—that alternative medicine can work in ways that traditional medicine cannot. Recently, the director of a major cancer hospital, whose own treatment program was failing to save him from his cancer, turned toward complementary medical treatment. He is now in remission and is opening up his own alternative medical center.

## All the Proof You Need

My experience in treating people with intractable problems has given me all the proof I need that this program works.

If you are overweight and you cleanse your system as well as work on your behavior, you will never need to diet again. I have seen this happen time and again. Weight comes off and blood pressure goes down, as do cholesterol and triglyceride levels. Body fat decreases while energy increases.

People can reverse most conditions without the need for traditional medical treatment. I've seen some breast cancers disappear, enlarged prostates shrink, and migraines, allergies, fibromyalgia, and emphysema alleviated through a natural healing program.

One participant in my program had such severe emphysema that he was on a respirator six times a day. He couldn't walk a block. Doctors at two separate hospitals advised, "You've got to have your left lung removed. If you do, you might live eight or nine months." He knew about my program and chose to pursue it instead—to great effect.

## Karen's Cure

Karen, a participant in one of my health support groups, suffered from a number of serious health problems, including kidney disease. Though her doctors said her problems were incurable, they suggested she take medications that would reduce her symptoms and keep them from progressing. She followed their instructions for eating a traditional diet, which included foods from the four food groups and consuming less fat. Nevertheless, she began to decline. Her kidney disease had caused retinopathy in both eyes, and her vision was getting worse. When she could no longer accept this further deterioration she decided to try something different and joined our program. She began the elimination, cleansing, and detoxification regimen. Everything she now did flew in the face of what her doctors had prescribed.

Karen's vision is now almost 20-20. She had suffered an infection in her toe that wouldn't heal for almost a year, despite antibiotic treatment. Her toe is now completely healed. She had had neuropathy in her hands and legs. The neuropathy is now completely gone. She had dangerously high blood pressure. It is now normal at 110/70. Her cholesterol level of 390 is now 211.

None of these dramatic changes were supposed to happen . . . not according to her doctors.

## Change Your Beliefs and Change Your Life

Several years ago, I performed an experiment. I ran a health support group for people who wanted to lose weight. I divided the group into five subgroups. The first group was put on a special diet; nothing else changed in their lives. Group two didn't change their diet, but they exercised more. Group three was given the best possible supplements and taught stress management. Group four was allowed to eat as before, minus the fat and sugar; they also took supplements. Group five was taught how to change their belief systems.

Which group do you think had the best results, stayed with the program, lost weight, and kept it off? It was group number five. Group five, the one that dealt only with values—and no longer valuing bad foods and a sedentary lifestyle, had the best results.

This proves that unless you address your beliefs you are going to have a difficult time sustaining any positive changes.

## Keep Growing

We so mistrust anything new because we don't trust our own critical mind. If something has never been done before, it is automatically suspect, unless we have the will and the desire to explore it for ourselves.

I can remember being stopped by the police twenty-five years ago. They thought I was a criminal because I was jogging in Central Park. I was running, and no one ran then unless it was away from someone. It seems I was just ahead of that curve of change.

## Being Open to the New

Being open to new ideas is one of the great gifts of life; it means you will always have the opportunity to change and grow. Growing means you're still alive; when you stop growing, you're dead. When faced with something new, be curious, ask questions, get to the bottom of it, and your life will expand in possibilities. When you have the information you need to make the decision to start this seven-step program, try those grains and juices, feel what eliminating sugar and caffeine will do for your well-being, and experience your own power in your freedom to choose.

When you reject out of hand anything new or different, you die—emotionally, creatively, and spiritually. Your vital *chi*, or life energy, ceases to pulse and radiate. You remain stuck, static. Each day becomes just like the one before, and you feel something vital is missing from your life. It's then that you become depressed, anxious, and unhealthy.

## Take the Right Risks

Karen learned a dynamic lesson: without risks there are no rewards. She dared to try something different, stayed with it, and got her life back.

When you take risks, make sure they are appropriate risks. If you are in critical condition and need emergency surgery, don't turn around and walk out of the hospital. All treatments have their place. To get the best care, you should be well informed about *all* your options.

Taking appropriate risks in life challenges our notions of who we thought we were and what we thought we could or couldn't do. When we take risks we break down barriers and strengthen our sense of self. Taking risks is liberating to both mind and body.

Angelo, a man in one of my groups, lost a hundred pounds. In order for him to give up meat and many of the foods he loved, he had to believe that there was another way of looking at his life and its possibilities. It took great strength—and great risk—for him to open his mind and challenge a lifetime of thinking of himself as a fat man. This man, who suffered from twelve serious conditions, is now healthy—and thin. Angelo's doctor said that his remission from hepatitis C was merely a coincidence, yet somehow this remission didn't occur during the nineteen years his doctor was treating him. Then, after one year of his being on my program, it happened. What a coincidence!

## Raise Your Expectations

The good news is, if you're reading this and thinking about these issues, you're awake. It may have taken a disease or some other crisis, but you realized that nothing would change if you didn't make it happen. And that's what matters. You now have the opportunity to make good choices. This becomes easier when you become truly conscious. You're going to focus on what you want to do, and you're going to set your goals. Remember, your performance can never exceed your own expectations. So you've got to *raise* your expectations—but not beyond what you know you can reasonably achieve. Set reasonable goals, and you will grow. If you slip, get back on track. But do it right. Each step you take will reward you first in your understanding of the principles behind the program, and then, little by little, by how much better you feel.

## Be Diligent, Be Patient

During the course of *The 7 Steps to Perfect Health* you'll find yourself on the same plane for a while until you become absolutely confident that you've mastered any particular step. Sometimes when we start a new program, we're initially inspired, and then, as we see that it takes discipline and commitment to stay the course, we begin to lose interest. By going slowly, you can avoid that problem. As you learn the rationale behind each step and see yourself becoming more knowledgeable about why you are doing what you are doing, you will continue to be inspired. Then you'll begin to grow again. You'll grow to a point, remain there until you become confident of what you can do, and then grow again. *The 7 Steps to Perfect Health* will not lead you to an overnight change. But perfect health will be yours—in time.

**AN INSPIRATIONAL STORY.**

A woman who followed my program found herself power walking daily. In less than two weeks, she and twenty others at my ranch were able to walk 26 miles in the hot sun in just one day. In fact, this woman had so much energy that she went an extra mile, walking 27 miles—a mile more than a marathon.

That's how much power the body has. You have that power. Think of how good you will feel when you use it.

## About the Author

Gary Null, the popular Pacifica Network talk show host, is a consumer advocate, investigative reporter, environmentalist and nutrition educator who has written more than 60 books on health topics. He says that, "You must be empowered before you can be whole," and he empowers his listeners with life-changing facts that promote wellness. Mr. Null has conducted over a hundred major investigations and has produced numerous documentaries in which he encourages his viewers to take charge of their lives and health. Among his dozens of videos are titles like "The Pain, Profit and Politics of AIDS," "Chronic Fatigue," "Diet for a Lifetime," and "Cancer: A Natural Approach." Gary Null lives the active, healthful life that he advocates. He regularly competes in races and marathons and has trained thousands of people in his "Natural Living Walking and Running Club" to do the same.

THE IBOOKS WEBSITE IS LOCATED AT
WWW.IBOOKSINC.COM

THE LIVEREADS WEBSITE IS LOCATED AT
WWW.LIVEREADS.COM

THE GARY NULL WEBSITE IS LOCATED AT
WWW.GARYNULL.COM

AN eBOOK VERSION OF THIS BOOK IS AVAILABLE
FROM ONLINE BOOKSELLERS